Edwin Louis C

Majoring in Men® | THE CURRICULUM FOR MEN

MAXIMIZED MANHOOD

A GUIDE TO FAMILY SURVIVAL

RESOLUTE BOOKS

Southlake, Texas

Unless otherwise indicated, all Scripture quotations are taken from the King James Version of the Holy Bible. Scripture quotations marked (AMP) are taken from the *Amplified® Bible*, © 1954, 1958, 1962, 1964, 1965, 1987 by The Lockman Foundation. Used by permission. (www.Lockman.org). Scripture quotations marked (NIV) are taken from the *Holy Bible, New International Version®*, NIV®, © 1973, 1978, 1984 by the International Bible Society. Used by permission of Zondervan. All rights reserved. Scripture quotations marked (TLB) are taken from *The Living Bible*, © 1971. Used by permission of Tyndale House Publishers, Inc., Wheaton, Illinois 60189. All rights reserved.

MAXIMIZED MANHOOD® WORKBOOK:
A Guide to Family Survival

Christian Men's Network
P.O. Box 3
Grapevine, TX 76099
www.CMN.men
Social:
@ChristianMensNetwork
@EdwinLouisCole
@PaulLouisCole

ISBN: 978-1-64123-129-9
Printed in the United States of America
© 2014 Edwin and Nancy Cole Legacy LLC

Published by:
Whitaker House
1030 Hunt Valley Circle
New Kensington, PA 15068

Majoring in Men® and Resolute Books™ are registered trademarks of Edwin and Nancy Cole Legacy LLC.

6 7 8 9 10 11 12 13 ⊔⊔ 28 27 26 25 24 23

TABLE OF CONTENTS

Lesson 1
Maximum Sentence
&
Kept Out of Canaan

Lesson 1
Maximum Sentence & Kept Out of Canaan

I.   Maximum Sentence (Chapter 1)

   A.   There were five reasons the Israelites didn't get into the Land of Promise. *(circle the five)*

   Read: *"Now these things were our examples, to the intent we should not lust after evil things, as they also lusted. Neither be ye idolaters, as were some of them; as it is written, The people sat down to eat and drink, and rose up to play. Neither let us commit fornication, as some of them committed, and fell in one day three and twenty thousand. Neither let us tempt Christ, as some of them also tempted, and were destroyed of serpents. Neither murmur ye, as some of them also murmured, and were destroyed of the destroyer"* 1 Corinthians 10:6-10.

   B.   Sex sins – A major problem among men

   Look up 2 Peter 3:3 and write out the verse.

   _____

   _____

   _____

For Further Study:

Lust – *"And the mixed multitude among them…began to lust greatly [for familiar and dainty food], and the Israelites wept again and said, Who will give us meat to eat?"* Numbers 11:4 AMP.

Idolatry – *"He [Aaron] took what they handed him and made it into an idol cast in the shape of a calf…he built an altar in front of the calf…the people rose early and sacrificed burnt offerings and presented fellowship offerings"* Exodus 32:4-6 NIV.

Fornication – *"While Israel was staying in Shittim, the men began to indulge in sexual immorality with Moabite women…those who died in the plague numbered 24,000"* Numbers 25:1, 9 NIV.

Tempting Christ – *"Ye shall not tempt the Lord your God, as ye tempted him in Massah"* Deuteronomy 6:16.

Murmuring – *"And the people murmured against Moses"* Exodus 15:25.

II. Kept Out of Canaan (Chapter 2)

A. God gives commands, not invitations.

Read: *"See, I have set before thee this day life and good, and death and evil; _____*

_____ thee this day to love the Lord thy God, to walk in His ways, and to keep his commandments and his statutes and his judgments, that thou mayest live and multiply: and the Lord thy God shall bless thee in the land whither thou goest to possess it" Deuteronomy 30:15-16.

B. Canaan Land

1. What does Canaan Land represent? *(page 20)*

_____

Who failed to reach Canaan? *(page 21)* _____

Who is able to enter Canaan Land today? *(page 21)* _____

In what areas of life can you experience Canaan Land? *(page 21)*

_____

For Further Study:

Commands – John 15:14; Acts 17:30; 1 Timothy 4:11

Canaan Land – *"For the Lord thy God bringeth thee into a good land, a land of brooks of water, of fountains and depths that spring out of the valleys and hills...A land wherein thou shalt eat bread without scarceness, thou shalt not lack anything in it...When thou hast eaten and art full, then thou shalt bless the Lord thy God for the good land which he hath given thee"* Deuteronomy 8:7-10.

Symbol of mankind's maximum potential – Deuteronomy 6:10-11

Where God's promises are fulfilled in our lives – Genesis 17:8; Galatians 3:29

Where we are to live – Genesis 13:15, 17; Deuteronomy 11:10-12

Where God wants us to live by faith today – Hebrews 4:1, 3; Galatians 3:7-11

Reality, not fantasy – Hebrews 3:15 TLB; Deuteronomy 12:9-11

Involves every area of life – Deuteronomy 12:7; 28:1-14; Romans 8:32

2. Read James 1:14-15.

    Define lust. *(page 21)* _____

    _____

3. Read Romans 1:21-23.
    What is the definition of idolatry? *(page 23)*

    A value system _____ in which we esteem something to be

    more worthy of our devotion than _____.

    Give five examples of idolatry you see every day. *(page 23)*

    _____

    _____

    _____

    _____

    _____

For Further Study:

Given to lust – *"But my people would not hearken to my voice…So I gave them up to their own hearts' lust: and they walked in their own counsels"* Psalm 81:11-12.

Preoccupation with self wants – Mark 4:18, 19; 1 Timothy 6:9; 2 Timothy 3:4; James 4:1-3; 1 John 2:16

Satisfaction/gratification of flesh – *"But put ye on the Lord Jesus Christ, and make no provisions for the flesh, to fulfill the lusts thereof"* Romans 13:14; 1 Corinthians 9:27.

Love gives; lust gets – 1 Corinthians 13:4, 5.

Idolatry – Ezekiel 14:3, 5; 20:15, 16; 44:10

Ego, prestige, popularity – *"Loved the praise of men"* John 12:43; Psalm 115:1-8; Herod: Acts 12:21-23

Money and business – *"A greedy person is really an idol worshiper—he loves and worships the good things of this life more than God"* Ephesians 5:5 TLB; Luke 12:16-20; Colossians 3:5 AMP.

Ministries – Acts 8:13-20

Pornography – *"Have you seen what the elders of the house of Israel do in the dark, every man in his [secret] chambers of [idol] pictures? For they say, The Lord does not see us"* Ezekiel 8:12; Romans 1:24-25.

4. Read 1 Corinthians 6:9-10.

Define fornication **in your own words.** *(page 24)*

_____

_____

Name a man in the Bible who committed fornication. *(page 24)* _____

What were the results of Israel committing fornication? *(page 25)* _____

_____

_____

For Further Study:

Fornication: every kind of sex sin – *"Don't you know that those doing such things have no share in the Kingdom of God? Don't fool yourselves. Those who live immoral lives, who are idol worshipers, adulterers or homosexuals— will have no share in his kingdom"* 1 Corinthians 6:9-10 TLB.

Godlessness – *"For people will be lovers of self and [utterly] self-centered, lovers of money and aroused by an inordinate [greedy] desire for wealth, proud and arrogant and contemptuous boasters. They will be abusive (blasphemous, scoffing), disobedient to parents, ungrateful, unholy and profane. [They will be] without natural [human] affection (callous and inhuman), relentless (admitting of no truce or appeasement); [they will be] slanderers (false accusers, troublemakers), intemperate and loose in morals and conduct, uncontrolled and fierce, haters of good. [They will be] treacherous [betrayers], rash, [and] inflated with self-conceit. [They will be] lovers of sensual pleasures and vain amusements more than and rather than lovers of God"* 2 Timothy 3:2 AMP.

Results of sex sins – Men of Israel: Numbers 25:1-4; Samson and Delilah: Judges 16:4-21; David and Bathsheba: 2 Samuel 11:1-12:12

5. Read Luke 4:9-12.

    If a man cheats on his taxes, can he expect God to bless him? *(page 25)*   ____ Yes ____ No

    Which sin is involved? *(circle one) (page 25)*
    lust   tempting Christ   pride

    Read 1 Corinthians 5:11.

    Review in your mind or discuss Numbers 12, the story of Miriam and Aaron murmuring against Moses.

    Can a "maximized man" associate with people who murmur? *(pages 25-26)*   ____ Yes ____ No

---

For Further Study:

Tempting Christ – *"And they sinned yet more against him by provoking the most High in the wilderness. And they tempted God in their heart by asking meat for their lust. Yea, they spake against God…Because they believed not in God, and trusted not in his salvation…How oft did they provoke him in the wilderness, and grieve him in the desert! Yea, they turned back and tempted God, and limited the Holy One of Israel"* Psalm 78:17-22, 31, 40, 41.

Lying and cheating and expecting God to bless – Jeremiah 23:26-33; Ananias and Sapphira: Acts 5:1-10

Murmuring – Negative confession: *"And ye murmured in your tents, and said, Because the Lord hated us, he hath brought us forth out of the land of Egypt, to deliver us into the hand of the Amorites, to destroy us"* Deuteronomy 1:27; *"These men are grumblers and faultfinders; they follow their own evil desires; they boast about themselves and flatter others for their own advantage"* Jude 16 NIV.

The tongue creates an uproar – *"The tongue also is a fire, a world of evil among the parts of the body. It corrupts the whole person, sets the whole course of his life on fire, and is itself set on fire by hell"* James 3:5, 6 NIV.

Practical:

Try to stop yourself five times this week from a sin that keeps men from being maximized. What is your weak point? *(not necessary to write down)*

Repeat this prayer out loud:

Father, in the Name of Jesus, I repent of lust, idolatry, fornication, tempting Christ and murmuring. I will keep Your commandments and walk in Your ways to be maximized in my manhood. I desire to live in Canaan and commit myself to continual repentance, study and application to achieve my maximum potential. Amen.

For Further Study:

Murmuring:

Against your boss – Miriam and Aaron: Numbers 12:1-15

Against spiritual leadership – *"The soul of the people was much discouraged because of the way. And the people spake against God, and against Moses…And the Lord sent fiery serpents among the people…and much people of Israel died"* Numbers 21:4-6.

Against God's Word – *"They despised the pleasant land, they believed not his word: But murmured in their tents, and hearkened not unto the voice of the Lord"* Psalm 106:24-26.

Consequences of murmuring – *"How long shall I bear with this evil congregation, which murmur against me? I have heard the murmurings of the children of Israel, which they murmur against me…Your carcases shall fall in this wilderness…in this wilderness they shall be consumed, and there they shall die"* Numbers 14:27-35.

Self-Test *Lesson 1*

1. What were the five sins that kept Israel out of Canaan?

    _____

    _____

    _____

    _____

    _____

2. Where is the passage of Scripture that talks about the five sins?

    _____

3. What is the definition of fornication?

    _____

    _____

4. What is the definition of lust?

    _____

5. James Smith dedicated his hardware store to God. He hired competent men for the front and hired inexpensive, illegal workers to stock the warehouse. His business was a constant struggle for him.

    Aside from anything outside this description that could have happened, what sin do you see he was guilty of?

    _____

    What results could he expect?

    _____

Keep this test for your own records.

Lesson 2
The Playboy Problem

Lesson 2
The Playboy Problem

A.   In this modern era, we can be guilty of "psychologizing" the Gospel.

In the process of psychologizing the Gospel, we eliminate the word _____ from our vocabulary.
(page 31)

B.   Read Psalm 32:3-5.

Sins have to be _____, _____ and _____.
(page 32)

C.   Read 1 Corinthians 5:11.

In your own words, if a brother in Christ maintains a lifestyle or habitual pattern of sin, what does the Bible have to say about our having fellowship with him? *(page 32)* _____

_____

_____

For Further Study:

All problems are somehow based on sin – *"Fools because of their transgression, and because of their iniquities, are afflicted"* Psalm 107:17; *"All unrighteousness is sin"* 1 John 5:17.

Confrontation and repentance – *"If we confess our sins, he is faithful and just to forgive us our sins, and to cleanse us from all unrighteousness"* 1 John 1:9; *"He that covereth his sins shall not prosper: but whoso confesseth and forsaketh them shall have mercy"* Proverbs 28:13.

Confess to the Lord – *"There was a time when I wouldn't admit what a sinner I was. But my dishonesty made me miserable...All day and all night your hand was heavy on me...Until I finally admitted all my sins to you and stopped trying to hide them. I said to myself, 'I will confess them to the Lord,' And you forgave me! All my guilt is gone"* Psalm 32:3-5 TLB.

D. Read 2 Corinthians 7:9-10.

What is the difference between human sorrow for sin and godly sorrow? *(page 33)*

_____

_____

_____

_____

We have been seduced into thinking that we have _____ instead of sin. *(page 33)*

E. If you surround a sinner with love and understanding, will his sin go away naturally? *(page 34)*
___ Yes ___ No

For Further Study:

Godly sorrow – *"Yet I am glad now, not because you were pained, but because you were pained into repentance [and so turned back to God]; for you felt a grief such as God meant you to feel, so that in nothing you might suffer loss through us or harm for what we did. For godly grief and the pain God is permitted to direct, produce a repentance that leads and contributes to salvation and deliverance from evil, and it never brings regret; but worldly grief (the hopeless sorrow that is characteristic of the pagan world) is deadly [breeding and ending in death]"*
2 Corinthians 7:9-10 AMP.

Seducing spirits/doctrines of devils blind us to truth – *"But the Holy Spirit tells us clearly that in the last times some in the church will turn away from Christ and become eager followers of teachers with devil-inspired ideas. These teachers will tell lies with straight faces and do it so often that their consciences won't even bother them"*
1 Timothy 4:1 TLB.

F.   Read Genesis 3:7-10 and Proverbs 28:13.

When it comes to sin, what is the major difference between human wisdom and godly wisdom?
(page 35) _____

_____

G.   Read John 15:14, and choose one answer to fill in the blank.

You are God's friend if you _____.

love Him   have faith in Him   obey Him

H.   Has humanity improved because of man's technical expertise? *(page 37)*
___ Yes ___ No

For Further Study:

Sin/hide/blame – *"I was afraid, because I was naked; and I hid myself...The woman whom thou gavest to be with me, she gave me of the tree, and I did eat"* Genesis 3:10, 12; *"If I covered my transgressions as Adam, by hiding mine iniquity in my bosom"* Job 31:33; *"There is a way which seemeth right unto a man, but the end thereof are the ways of death"* Proverbs 14:12.

Sin/confess/mercy – *"A man who refuses to admit his mistakes can never be successful. But if he confesses and forsakes them, he gets another chance"* Proverbs 28:13 TLB.

Human wisdom – *"They are all gone aside, they are all together become filthy: there is none that doeth good, no, not one"* Psalm 14:3; *"Hath not God made foolish the wisdom of this world"* 1 Corinthians 1:20, 21; *"The Lord knoweth the thoughts of the wise, that they are vain"* 1 Corinthians 3:20; *"If any man think that he knoweth any thing, he knoweth nothing yet as he ought to know"* 1 Corinthians 8:2; *"But if ye have bitter envying and strife in your hearts, glory not, and lie not against the truth. This wisdom descendeth not from above, but is earthly, sensual, devilish. For where envying and strife is, there is confusion and every evil work"* James 3:13-16.

I.   Look up James 3:17 and write out the attributes of godly wisdom.

1.   _____

2.   _____

3.   _____

4.   _____

5.   _____

6.   _____

7.   _____

J.   Fill in the blanks. *(page 37)*

Human wisdom will never lead us into our _____ Land.

You can never maximize your potential until you have received _____.

Sweethearts living together out of wedlock are really _____.

For Further Study:

Godly wisdom – *"These are the laws you must obey…You will no longer go your own way as you do now, everyone doing whatever he thinks is right"* Deuteronomy 12:1, 8 TLB; *"But the wisdom that comes from heaven is first of all pure and full of quiet gentleness. Then it is peace-loving and courteous. It allows discussion and is willing to yield to others; it is full of mercy and good deeds. It is wholehearted and straightforward and sincere"* James 3:17 TLB. Conquer sin – *"Why is your face so dark with rage? It can be bright with joy if you will do what you should! But if you refuse to obey, watch out. Sin is waiting to attack you, longing to destroy you. But you can conquer it!"* Genesis 4:6, 7; *"Do not let sin control your puny body any longer; do not give in to its sinful desires. Do not let any part of your bodies become tools of wickedness, to be used for sinning; but give yourselves completely to God— every part of you—for you are back from death and you want to be tools in the hands of God, to be used for his good purposes"* Romans 6:12, 13.

Practical:

1. What are some areas of your life that you've labeled as "problems" rather than "sin"?

   _____

   _____

2. 1 Corinthians 15:33 NIV tells us, *"Do not be misled: Bad company corrupts good character."* What relationships with others might be bringing wrong influences into your life? *(write out here or use a separate sheet)*

   _____

   _____

   _____

For Further Study:

Choices determine conduct, character and destiny –

"I want the company of the godly men and women in the land; they are the true nobility" Psalm 16:3 TLB.

"My son, if sinners entice you, do not give in to them. If they say, 'Come along with us…throw in your lot with us'…do not go along with them, do not set foot on their paths; for their feet rush in to sin, they are swift to shed blood" Proverbs 1:10 NIV; *"Run from anything that gives you the evil thoughts that young men often have, but stay close to anything that makes you want to do right"* 2 Timothy 2:22 TLB.

"A good man is known by his truthfulness; a false man by deceit and lies…No real harm befalls the good, but there is constant trouble for the wicked" Proverbs 12:17, 21 TLB.

"Be with wise men and become wise. Be with evil men and become evil" Proverbs 13:20 TLB; *"He who walks with the wise grows wise, but a companion of fools suffers harm"* Proverbs 13:20 NIV.

"A good name is rather to be chosen than great riches, and loving favour rather than silver and gold" Proverbs 22:1.

3. Read out loud: *"The law of the Lord is perfect, converting the soul: the testimony of the Lord is sure, making wise the simple. The statutes of the Lord are right, rejoicing the heart: the commandment of the Lord is pure, enlightening the eyes. The fear of the Lord is clean, enduring for ever: the judgments of the Lord are true and righteous altogether. More to be desired are they than gold, yea, than much fine gold: sweeter also than honey and the honeycomb. Moreover by them is thy servant warned: and in keeping of them there is great reward. Who can understand his errors? cleanse thou me from secret faults. Keep back thy servant also from presumptuous sins; let them not have dominion over me: then shall I be upright, and I shall be innocent from the great transgression. Let the words of my mouth, and the meditation of my heart, be acceptable in thy sight, O Lord, my strength, and my redeemer"* Psalm 19:7-14.

Repeat this prayer out loud:

Father, in the Name of Jesus, reveal to my heart the areas that I have tried to cover up, that are offensive to You. As You reveal them to me, I will be faithful to repent of them and put them behind me. Forgive me for leaning on human wisdom and compromising my way, rather than being strong and quick to obey Your will. As the psalmist said, keep my soul away from presumptuous sin. I will walk before You with an honest heart. Amen.

Principles I want to memorize:

Self-Test *Lesson 2*

1. Human sorrow for sin is based on being _____, while godly

    sorrow is based on _____.

2. What is the passage of Scripture that admonishes us not to fellowship, even have lunch, with an individual

    who wants to hold to his lifestyle of sin? _____

3. The Watergate scandal in Washington, D.C., years ago, was a classic example of what?

    Man's desire to _____ his sin

4. What does God expect us to do about our sin(s)?

    _____

Keep this test for your own records.

Lesson 3
Moses and the Ten Invitations

Lesson 3
Moses and the Ten Invitations

A. God commands us to love. *(page 40)*

Write out John 13:34-35. _____

_____

_____

Love centers in the will. That is why love can be commanded and why God can command love. In what areas of your life do you personally need to go beyond your "feelings" and love anyway?

_____

_____

B. Look up Romans 5:8. *"But God commendeth His love toward us, in that,* _____

_____, *Christ died for us."*

C. God delights in taking "death" and bringing it into "life." Part of God's "job description" is that He raises from the dead. Read John 11:34-44. What areas of your life, business or marriage need resurrection?

_____

For Further Study:

Commanded to love – *"Jesus said unto him, Thou shalt love the Lord thy God with all thy heart, and with all thy soul, and with all thy mind. This is the first and great commandment. And the second is like unto it, Thou shalt love thy neighbour as thyself. On these two commandments hang all the law and the prophets"* Matthew 22:37-40; *"The goal of this command is love, which comes from a pure heart and a good conscience and a sincere faith"*
1 Timothy 1:5 NIV.
A difference between passion and love – Tamar and Amnon: 2 Samuel 13:1-19
Real love is always good – *"Love worketh no ill to his neighbour: therefore love is the fulfilling of the law"* Romans 13:10; *"Let every one of us please his neighbour for his good to edification"* Romans 15:2.
Love centers in the will and can be commanded – *"I will love thee, O Lord, my strength"* Psalm 18:1.

D. Read: *"And the times of this ignorance God winked at; but now* _____
all men every where to repent: Because he hath appointed a day, in the which he will judge the world in
righteousness by that man whom he hath ordained; whereof he hath given assurance unto all men, in that
he hath raised him from the dead" Acts 17:30-31.

E. Fill in the blanks. *(pages 42–43)*

1. When you are given an invitation, you can either _____ it or _____ it.

2. When you are given a command, you can only _____ or _____.

F. List three ways that obedience to God will maximize a man. *(page 44)*

1. _____

2. _____

3. _____

G. Obedience brings _____. Disobedience shatters it. In its place, it will bring confusion,
pain and suffering. *(page 44)*

For Further Study:

Commanded to repent – *"And that repentance and remission of sins should be preached in his name among all
nations, beginning at Jerusalem"* Luke 24:47.
Obeying God maximizes manhood – *"If ye be willing and obedient, ye shall eat the good of the land"* Isaiah 1:19.
Obeying God brings peace – *"My son, forget not my law; but let thine heart keep my commandments: For length of
days, and long life, and peace, shall they add to thee"* Proverbs 3:1, 2; *"Great peace have they which love thy law:
and nothing shall offend them"* Psalm 119:165.
Disobedience shatters peace – *"There is no peace, saith my God, to the wicked"* Isaiah 57:21; *"The way of peace
they know not; and there is no judgment in their goings: they have made them crooked paths: whosoever goeth
therein shall not know peace"* Isaiah 59:8.
No disobedient spirit in Heaven – *"Know ye not that the unrighteous shall not inherit the kingdom of God? Be not
deceived: neither fornicators, nor idolaters, nor adulterers, nor effeminate, nor abusers of themselves with mankind.
Nor thieves, nor covetous, nor drunkards, nor revilers, nor extortioners, shall inherit the kingdom of God"*
1 Corinthians 6:9, 10; Galatians 5:19-21; Revelation 22:14, 15.

H. God commands confession—confession to get rid of sin; confession to put on righteousness. Repentance *from* sin and faith *toward* God is the balance. *(page 46)*

Write out Proverbs 28:13.

_____

_____

I. Unconfessed sin is unforgiven sin. Sin can come out of the life only through: *(circle one) (page 46)*

the heart   the mouth   groaning

J. People are looking for truth. People are looking for reality. *(page 47)*

1. Truth and reality are _____.

2. Truth must be spoken in _____.

Many people are afraid of speaking the truth, afraid of hurting others or losing their love. They don't realize that truth, spoken in love, is the only way to show real love. *(page 47)*

"Backwards loving" can be called "best affections." Give an example of hurting someone by means of "best affections" from something you've seen or experienced in your own life.

_____

_____

For Further Study:

Confession to get rid of sin – *"If we confess our sins, he is faithful and just to forgive us our sins, and to cleanse us from all unrighteousness"* 1 John 1:9.

Unconfessed sin is unforgiven sin – Parable of the Pharisee and the publican: Luke 18:9-14.

Truth spoken in love – *"But speaking the truth in love, may grow up into him in all things, which is the head, even Christ"* Ephesians 4:15

Perversion of best affections – David and Absalom: 2 Samuel 19:1-7

K. Godly sorrow is necessary for repentance. Sorrow is one of life's greatest teachers. *(page 50)*
Write out Ecclesiastes 7:3.

_____

_____

You'll never know the joy of *graduation* until you've experienced the sorrow of *studying*.
You'll never know the joy of a *paycheck* until you've experienced the sorrow of **getting up in the morning for work**.

You'll never know the joy of **winning a race** until you've experienced the sorrow of **practice**.

Give two more examples **in your own words** of sorrow bringing you to joy.

You'll never know the joy of _____ until you've experienced the sorrow of _____.
You'll never know the joy of _____ until you've experienced the sorrow of _____.

For Further Study:

Godly sorrow is necessary to repentance – *"For godly sorrow worketh repentance to salvation not to be repented of: but the sorrow of the world worketh death"* 2 Corinthians 7:10; Psalm 51.
Sorrow a great teacher – *"It is good for me that I have been afflicted; that I might learn thy statutes"* Psalm 119:71.
Conviction leads to repentance, not hurt – *"Oh, that there were such an heart in them, that they would fear me, and keep all my commandments always, that it might be well with them, and with their children for ever!"*
Deuteronomy 5:29; *"Yet, when we are judged and punished by the Lord, it is so that we will not be condemned with the rest of the world"* 1 Corinthians 11:32 TLB; *"Cast away from you all your transgressions...and make you a new heart and a new spirit: for why will ye die...For I have no pleasure in the death of him that dieth, saith the Lord God: wherefore turn yourselves, and live ye"* Ezekiel 18:31-32; Ephesians 2:1-6; Colossians 1:21, 22.

Practical:

1. Name a time in your life when you tried to share truth but without much love.

    _____

    _____

    When have you tried to share truth, speaking in love?

    _____

    _____

    Was there any difference in response? _____

    _____

2. Think over your own responses to people who have spoken truth to you. How do you receive advice or correction? _____

    _____

    What can you do to accept the truth, spoken in love, from those who love you and want to help you?

    _____

    _____

For Further Study:

God loves the sinner but hates the sin –

"But God commendeth his love toward us, in that, while we were yet sinners, Christ died for us" Romans 5:8.

"I know you get no pleasure from wickedness and cannot tolerate the slightest sin" Psalm 5:4 TLB.

"Don't plot harm to others; don't swear that something is true when it isn't! How I hate all that sort of thing! says the Lord" Zechariah 8:17 TLB.

3.   Man whitewashes; God washes white. *(page 52)*
Read aloud: *"Woe to you, teachers of the law and Pharisees, you hypocrites! You are like whitewashed tombs, which look beautiful on the outside but on the inside are full of dead men's bones and everything unclean. In the same way, on the outside you appear to people as righteous but on the inside you are full of hypocrisy and wickedness"* Matthew 23:27-28 NIV.

Repeat this prayer out loud:

Father, in Jesus' Name, help me to have an open mind and heart when others come to me. Forgive me for bad attitudes. Help me to receive Your love into my heart before I speak words of truth. I make the decision today to follow the commandment to love, that I may be seen as a disciple of Christ. Amen.

For Further Study:

God washes white – *"Though your sins be as scarlet, they shall be as white as snow; though they be red like crimson, they shall be as wool"* Isaiah 1:18; *"Therefore if any man be in Christ, he is a new creature; old things are passed away; behold, all things are become new"* 2 Corinthians 5:17; *"These are they which came out of great tribulation, and have washed their robes, and made them white in the blood of the Lamb"* Revelation 7:14.
Confession to put on righteousness –
"That if thou shalt confess with thy mouth the Lord Jesus, and shalt believe in thine heart that God hath raised him from the dead, thou shalt be saved. For with the heart man believeth unto righteousness; and with the mouth confession is made unto salvation" Romans 10:9, 10; *"Whosoever therefore shall confess me before men, him will I confess also before my Father which is in heaven"* Matthew 10:32; *"Anyone who confesses (acknowledges, owns) that Jesus is the Son of God, God abides (lives, makes His home) in him, and he [abides, lives, makes his home] in God"* 1 John 4:15 AMP.

Self-Test *Lesson 3*

1.   Are God's commandments *absolutes* or *negotiable*? _____

2.   **In your own words**, write out the key difference between commandments and invitations.

    _____

    _____

    _____

3.   When a man obeys God, it _____ his manhood.

4.   Lucifer is an example of a _____ spirit. He was immediately expelled from Heaven.

5.   Parents often find situations where they want to deliver their children from the consequences of their actions and disobedience. Doing this can cause the child to feel free to repeat his actions.

    Parents who fall into this category can be said to be guilty of _____, or a kind of "backwards loving."

Keep this test for your own records.

Lesson 4

There's a Hole in the Door
&
Tender and Tough

Lesson 4

There's a Hole in the Door & Tender and Tough

I.   There's a Hole in the Door (Chapter 5)

   A.   Forgiveness is always a release. *(page 55)* Write out Psalm 103:12.

   _____

   _____

   Men need to learn forgiveness. Look up Ephesians 4:32. *"And be ye kind one to another, tenderhearted,*
   _____, *even as God for Christ's sake hath*

   _____ *you."*

   B.   Unforgiveness binds you to one who has wronged you. Unforgiveness toward an abusive parent can often birth the same sin in you. *(page 57)*

   1.   Read: *"Whosesoever sins ye remit, they are remitted unto them; and whosesoever sins ye retain, they are retained"* John 20:23.

   2.   Name people in your life whom you have not forgiven *(you may use a separate sheet).*

   _____

   _____

For Further Study:

God releases from repented sins – *"I, even I, am he that blotteth out thy transgressions for mine own sake, and will not remember thy sins"* Isaiah 43:25; *"For I will forgive their iniquity, and I will remember their sin no more"* Jeremiah 31:34; Acts 5:31; Ephesians 1:7; Colossians 1:14.

Men need to learn this type forgiveness – *"And when ye stand praying, forgive, if ye have aught against any: that your Father...in heaven may forgive you your trespasses"* Mark 11:25; *"Forbearing one another, and forgiving one another, if any man have a quarrel against any: even as Christ forgave you, so also do ye"* Colossians 3:13.

Unforgiveness restrains – *"For if ye forgive men their trespasses, your heavenly Father will also forgive you: But if ye forgive not men their trespasses, neither will your Father forgive your trespasses"* Matthew 6:14, 15.

Unforgiveness binds you to your offender – Moses and children of Israel: Numbers 20:2-12; Psalm 106:32, 33.

Unforgiveness can transcend generations – 2 Chronicles 10:19.

3. Review your list carefully. Are you, in any way, reaping what they sowed? *(not necessary to write down)*

C. It is part of maximized manhood, and it is _____ to give and receive forgiveness. *(page 60)*

D. Sins are often passed from generation to generation, because they are: *(circle one) (page 60)*

    inherited   genetically-based   not forgiven

II. Tender and Tough (Chapter 6)

A. Balance is the key to life; therefore, men must learn to be both _____ and _____. *(page 63)*

    List three ideas of how balance can be kept when dealing with children. *(page 63)*

    _____

    _____

    _____

For Further Study:

Christlike to forgive and receive forgiveness – *"Then said Jesus, Father, forgive them; for they know not what they do"* Luke 23:34; *"And he (Stephen) kneeled down, and cried with a loud voice, Lord, lay not this sin to their charge. And when he had said this, he fell asleep"* Acts 7:60.

Sins passed from generation to generation – *"Those left shall pine away in enemy lands because of their sins, the same sins as those of their fathers"* Leviticus 26:39 TLB.

Leadership in the home – *"He that spareth his rod hateth his son: but he that loveth him chasteneth him betimes"* Proverbs 13:24; *"And, ye fathers, provoke not your children to wrath: but bring them up in the nurture and admonition of the Lord"* Ephesians 6:4.

Discipline begins with self – Paul: *"I punish my body...training it to do what it should, not what it wants to"* 1 Corinthians 9:26, 27; Mark 9:43-48; Hebrews 6:12.

Undisciplined love can destroy –
David after Absalom's death: 2 Samuel 19:1-6; Samson and Delilah: Judges 16:4-31.

B. Think of Bible stories you know, and list a few examples of Jesus' tenderness.

_____

_____

C. The highest good of every individual is to be like Jesus, so manhood and Christlikeness are synonymous. *(page 65)*

Look up Romans 8:29. *"For whom he did foreknow, he also did predestinate to be conformed to the _____ of his Son, that he might be the firstborn among many brethren."*

D. Read: *"I am the true vine, and my Father is the gardener. He cuts off every branch in me that bears no fruit, while every branch that does bear fruit he prunes so that it will be even more fruitful"* John 15:1-2 NIV.

1. The fruit God expects from our lives as men is: *(see Luke 13:6-9) (circle one) (page 66)*

   angelic character   manhood   hard work

For Further Study:

Jesus was the perfect balance of tender and tough –

Tender: Matthew 19:13-15;   Tough: Luke 8:22-25; 11:37-52;
         Mark 6:34; John 14:27;   John 2:13-17; 1 John 3:8;
         Romans 5:8; 1 John 3:16   Revelation 19:15

Be like Jesus – *"Till we all come in the unity of the faith, and of the knowledge of the Son of God, unto a perfect man, unto the measure of the stature of the fullness of Christ"* Ephesians 4:13.

Have the Word in you – Psalm 119:9, 11; John 1:14; *"The whole Bible was given to us by inspiration from God and is useful to teach us what is true and to make us realize what is wrong in our lives; it straightens us out and helps us do what is right"* 2 Timothy 3:16 TLB; *"My words abide in you...ye bear much fruit"* John 15:7, 8.

Belonging to God results in manhood – *"I have chosen you, and ordained you, that ye should go and bring forth fruit, and that your fruit should remain"* John 15:16.

2. Jesus effectively said in John 15:2, *"If it doesn't produce, _____!"* *(page 66)*

E. The Kingdom of God is based on truth, not on human _____. *(page 67)*

F. Read Joshua 24:15.

Women desire their men to make _____. *(page 71)*

G. Maturity doesn't come with age but with the acceptance of _____. *(page 72)*

H. No one can be responsible for success unless he is willing to accept the responsibility for: *(circle one) (page 72)*

his wife   money   failure

I. The more Word you have in you, the more _____ you become. *(page 74)*

For Further Study:

Produce results or be cut off – *"Bring forth therefore fruits worthy of repentance"* Luke 3:7-9.

Repent of and forsake dead works – *"Therefore leaving the principles of the doctrine of Christ, let us go on unto perfection; not laying again the foundation of repentance from dead works, and of faith toward God"* Hebrews 6:1.

Truth, not sentiment – *"Jesus saith unto him, I am the way, the truth, and the life: no man cometh unto the Father, but by me"* John 14:6; 1 Thessalonians 2:13.

Accept responsibility for decisions in order to mature – *"And David was the youngest: and the three eldest followed Saul…And David said to Saul, Let no man's heart fail because of him; thy servant will go and fight with this Philistine"* 1 Samuel 17:14, 32; Jacob: Genesis 32-33 AMP; Gideon: Judges 6-8; *"His lord said unto him, Well done, good and faithful servant; thou hast been faithful over a few things, I will make thee ruler over many things: enter thou into the joy of thy lord"* Matthew 25:23.

Success rests on accepting responsibility for failure – *"He that covereth his sins shall not prosper: but whoso confesseth and forsaketh them shall have mercy"* Proverbs 28:13.

J. What changed the prodigal? *(circle all that apply) (page 75)*

new clothes   accepting responsibility for his actions

repentance   the fatted calf

asking for forgiveness   pigs

Practical:

1. If we fail to act in truth because of sentiment, the consequences can be tragic.

    a. Read 1 Samuel 2:12-36 and 3:13, 14 about Eli and his sons.

    b. List times when you've been guilty of acting on sentiment rather than truth.

    _____

    _____

For Further Study:

Decision making is a mark of a man – *"Choose you this day whom ye will serve…but as for me and my house, we will serve the Lord"* Joshua 24:15.

Admit, repent and learn from wrong decisions – Jonah 2-3; The Prodigal: Luke 15:11-24.

Forget your forgiven past – *"Forgetting those things which are behind, and reaching forth unto those things which are before, I press toward the mark for the prize of the high calling of God in Christ Jesus"* Philippians 3:13, 14; *"And Jesus said unto him, No man, having put his hand to the plough, and looking back, is fit for the kingdom of God"* Luke 9:62; Romans 8:30-39.

Decision based on selfish gratification – *"From whence come wars and fightings among you? come they not hence, even of your lusts that war in your members?...Ye ask, and receive not, because ye ask amiss, that ye may consume it upon your lusts"* James 4:1-3; Pilate and Barabbas: Matthew 27:20-24.

Decision by default – *"He that is not with me is against me; and he that gathereth not with me scattereth abroad"* Matthew 12:30.

2. Consider the types of wrong decisions mentioned on page 71.

    Decisions based on personal preferences or selfish gratification, rather than what is best for the followers

    No decision (a decision by default)

    Indecisiveness (which creates instability)

    Reflect back and name times when you were guilty of each.

    Which of these three most affects you? *(not necessary to write down)*

    What can you do about it?

    What will you do about it this week?

Repeat this prayer out loud:

Father, You know my heart, and You see what I'm writing on these pages. I ask You to help me accept responsibility and become truly mature in every area of my manhood. I submit to You my errors of the past, thank You for Your forgiveness and ask You to help me go forward with good balance, good decisions and a better relationship with You and all those around me. Amen.

For Further Study:

Indecisiveness – *"A double minded man is unstable in all his ways"* James 1:8; *"Elijah…said, How long halt ye between two opinions? if the Lord be God, follow him: but if Baal, then follow him. And the people answered him not a word"* 1 Kings 18:21; They profess to hate sin but have a lingering love for it – James 4:1; They lack a right understanding of good and evil – Hebrews 5:14.

Make a decision – *"I have refrained my feet from every evil way, that I might keep thy word. I have not departed from thy judgments: for thou hast taught me…Through thy precepts I get understanding: therefore I hate every false way"* Psalm 119:101, 102, 104; *"And Solomon determined to build an house for the name of the Lord"* 2 Chronicles 2:1; *"Write the vision, and make it plain upon tables, that he may run that readeth it"* Habakkuk 2:2. Dedication and discipline enable you to overcome all obstacles – Isaiah 50:7; *"For Ezra had prepared his heart to seek the law of the Lord, and to do it, and to teach in Israel statues and judgments"* Ezra 7:10.

Self-Test *Lesson 4*

1. Leadership in the home requires both _____ and _____.

2. Unforgiveness _____ you to the sin of the one who has wronged you.

3. Sins are inherited. ___ True ___ False

4. There are times when God requires you to be "rough" in your leadership at home. ___ True ___ False

5. Our God looks for fruitfulness in our lives. The fruit He expects from us is manhood.
   One of the principles of the Kingdom is, if it isn't producing, _____.

6. The major issue in becoming "mature" in our manhood is learning to _____
   _____ for our decisions.

7. What are some areas in which I need to be tougher on myself?
   _____
   _____

8. What are some areas in which I need to be more tender with those I lead?
   _____
   _____

9. What are some areas in which I need to be more decisive?
   _____
   _____

Keep this test for your own records.

Lesson 5

Is There a Priest in the House?
&
The One-Dollar Tip

Lesson 5

Is There a Priest in the House? & The One-Dollar Tip

I.   Is There a Priest in the House? (Chapter 7)

    A.   The priest ministers not only to the Lord but also to the ones entrusted to his care. *(page 76)*
       In your own words, what are major areas of your life that you are responsible for as a minister?

       _____

       _____

    B.   As priest of the home, you must pray with and for your wife. *(page 78)*

       1.   You become _____ with the one *to* whom you pray, the one *for* whom you pray
           and the one *with* whom you pray.

       2.   Prayer produces _____.

    C.   Sexual relations are one thing; _____ is another. If you
       really want to be one with your wife, then pray for her and with her. *(page 79)*

       Read: *"Can two walk together, except they _____?"* Amos 3:3.

    D.   Some women try to play God. Read 2 Samuel 6:20-23—David and Michal.

For Further Study:

Ministry – *"All Scripture is given by inspiration of God, and is profitable…That the man of God may be perfect, thoroughly furnished unto all good works"* 2 Timothy 3:16, 17; Ministry to the Lord: Exodus 28:1; Ministry to your wife: Ephesians 5:25-29; Ministry to your children: Ephesians 6:4.

Prayer produces intimacy – To whom you pray: The Lord and Moses: Exodus 33:11; For whom you pray: *"When I pray for you…Only God knows how deep is my love and longing for you with the tenderness of Jesus Christ"* Philippians 1:1-8 TLB; With whom you pray: Acts 2:42, 45-47.

Prayer agreement brings power – *"If two of you shall agree on earth as touching any thing that they shall ask, it shall be done for them of my Father which is in heaven"* Matthew 18:19; *"They raised their voices together in prayer to God…And when they had prayed, the place was shaken where they were assembled together; and they were all filled with the Holy Ghost, and they spake the word of God with boldness"* Acts 4:24-31.

1. Write out John 6:44.

   _____

   _____

2. Who draws a man to God? *(page 81)* _____

3. A woman needs to _____ her husband for his sins and love _____. *(pages 81–82)*

E. Men can change _____. Only God can change a _____. *(page 81)*

   Read: *"Therefore if any man be in Christ, he is a _____: old things are passed away; behold, all things are become new"* 2 Corinthians 5:17.

F. A man ministers to his wife by giving her assurance.

   1. Every woman needs to know she is _____ to her man. *(page 82)*

   2. Read Proverbs 31:28.

      In your own words, describe how you can minister to a wife's uniqueness.

      _____

      _____

   3. You are _____ to what you confess. *(page 83)*

For Further Study:

Only God can change a man's nature – John 1:12, 13.

Keys for women –

Forgive: *"[Now having received the Holy Spirit, and being led and directed by Him] if you forgive the sins of anyone, they are forgiven; if you retain the sins of anyone, they are retained"* John 20:23; *"Forbearing one another, and forgiving one another, if any man have a quarrel against any: even as Christ forgave you, so also do ye"* Colossians 3:13; Parable of the unforgiving servant: Matthew 18:23-30; *"When ye stand praying, forgive, if ye have aught against any"* Mark 11:25, 26.

Love: *"Love never fails"* 1 Corinthians 13:8 NIV; 1 Peter 3:1, 2.

Women need to know they are unique – *"Rejoice with the wife of thy youth…be thou ravished always with her love"* Proverbs 5:18-20; Song of Solomon.

G.   Everything in life is _____. *(page 84)*

H.   You are only a _____ of your wife's love, not a possessor of it. *(page 85)*

I.   Look up 1 Timothy 3:5. What is a man's main priority? *(circle one)*
     church
     earning a living
     ministering to his family

J.   Read: *"Moreover it is required in stewards, that a man be found _____"*
     1 Corinthians 4:2.

II.   The One-Dollar Tip (Chapter 8)
     A.   Write out 1 Peter 3:7.

     _____

     _____

     _____

For Further Study:

Confess certainty about your spouse – *"A double minded man is unstable in all his ways"* James 1:8; *"So ought men to love their wives as their own bodies. He that loveth his wife loveth himself. For no man ever yet hated his own flesh; but nourisheth and cherisheth it…a man…shall be joined unto his wife, and they two shall be one flesh"* Ephesians 5:28-31.

Men are only stewards – *"And the Lord God took the man, and put him into the garden of Eden to dress it and to keep it"* Genesis 2:15; *"The earth is the Lord's, and the fulness thereof; the world, and they that dwell therein"* Psalm 24:1.

Men are accountable for their stewardship – *"So then every one of us shall give account of himself to God"* Romans 14:12; *"For other foundation can no man lay than that is laid, which is Jesus Christ. Now if any man build upon this foundation…Every man's work shall be made manifest…because it shall be revealed by fire; and the fire shall try every men's work of what sort it is"* 1 Corinthians 3:11-15.

1. If you do not treat your wife right, your _____ will not get ready answers. *(page 89)*

2. **In your own words,** name some effects in life that can come from God not answering you.

   _____

   _____

B. Assumption is life's _____ level of knowledge. *(page 91)*

C. Self-justification makes you right in _____ eyes by placing _____ on someone else. *(page 91)*

D. When the man treats his wife like chattel instead of a joint heir, the _____ observe it and reflect the same attitude in their actions. *(page 92)*

E. When something _____, it gains in value. *(page 92)*

   When something _____, it loses in value. *(page 92)*

For Further Study:

Treat your wife correctly – *"Because the Lord hath been witness between thee and the wife of thy youth, against whom thou hast dealt treacherously: yet is she thy companion, and the wife of thy covenant. And did not he make one?...That he might seek a godly seed. Therefore take heed to your spirit, and let none deal treacherously against the wife of his youth"* Malachi 2:13-15.

A married man cannot live independently of his wife – *"Therefore shall a man...cleave unto his wife: and they shall be one flesh"* Genesis 2:24; *"But at the beginning of creation God 'made them male and female.' 'For this reason a man will leave his father and mother and be united to his wife, and the two will become one flesh.' So they are no longer two, but one. Therefore what God has joined together, let man not separate"* Mark 10:6-8 NIV.

Everything in life appreciates or depreciates – *"It is naught, it is naught, saith the buyer: but when he is gone his way, then he boasteth"* Proverbs 20:14; Parable of the Sower and Soils: Mark 4:8-19.

F. When a woman is appreciated, she gains value in: *(circle as many as apply)* *(page 93)*

your eyes

her eyes

her children's eyes

G. What positive attributes can you say your wife has, even if only partially? *(circle all that apply)*

good spirit	loyalty	responds to love
hospitality	good mother	attention to detail
steady worker	desire for goodness	retains friendships
devotion	humor	future-minded

How can you bring out her strengths? _____

_____

Practical:

1. What are some specific areas where you can strengthen your position as the priest of your home?

_____

_____

_____

_____

For Further Study:

Pitfall of marriage #1: Assumption – *"Therefore my people are gone into captivity, because they have no knowledge: and their honourable men are famished, and their multitude dried up with thirst"* Isaiah 5:13; *"My people are destroyed for lack of knowledge"* Hosea 4:6; Job 35:16.

Pitfall of marriage #2: Self-justification – Adam blaming Eve: *"The man said, The woman whom thou gavest to be with me, she gave me of the tree, and I did eat"* Genesis 3:9-13; Ahab blaming Elijah: *"When Ahab saw Elijah… Ahab said unto him, Art thou he that troubleth Israel? And he answered, I have not troubled Israel; but thou, and thy father's house, in that ye have forsaken the commandments of the Lord"* 1 Kings 18:17, 18.

2. Think about your family life, and write down some thoughts on paper. THEN, go to your wife and ask her to join you in prayer for those matters. Don't promise to do it regularly. Just DO IT regularly. *(Sometimes she cannot hear your words because your actions are too loud!)*

3. Look your wife in the eyes TODAY, and tell her how special she is to you.

4. Plan your next "honeymoon" now, spending at least one night away from home.

5. Have you allowed yourself to make jokes about your wife? *(not necessary to write down)* Are there areas of her life that you habitually murmur about, even though joking? What can you say in place of such jokes? Write out appropriate phrases to say to your wife regularly. Commit them to memory. And commit to the Lord to use them.

_____

_____

_____

Repeat this prayer out loud:

Father, in Jesus' Name, forgive me for not being a priest in my home. Help me be faithful to come to You and then faithful to go to my wife. Forgive me for prayerlessness in the home. I make the decision today to be a man of prayer and a tender, but firm, priest in my home. Open my eyes to ways I can minister to my wife, and help me be faithful to minister to her daily. I desire for my wife to be completely comfortable around me. I want her to know that she is safe when I'm around, especially when we are with others. Please forgive me for knowingly or unknowingly hurting my wife by my choice of words and jokes. Help me to listen to her and to value what she says, even when I don't agree. I determine right now to build up my wife, not only when we are in public but also when we are all alone. I ask You to help me achieve these goals so that our marriage brings glory to You. Thank You, Father. Amen.

Principles I want to memorize:

Self-Test *Lesson 5*

1. As the priest of the home, I minister not only to the Lord but also to _____ _____.

2. Prayer produces _____.

3. Every woman needs to know she is _____.

4. Ministry is defined as preaching.   ___ True ___ False

5. **In your own words,** in what areas of life is a man responsible to minister?

    _____

    _____

    _____

6. A man never stops ministering.   ___ True ___ False

7. Fill in the blank from memory.
    "Likewise, ye husbands, dwell with them according to knowledge, giving honour unto the wife, as unto the weaker vessel, and as being heirs together of the grace of life; _____ *be not hindered"* 1 Peter 3:7.

8. One of the lowest levels of knowledge is _____.

9. Children will pick up from _____ their attitude toward their mother.

10. Murmuring against your wife will keep you from having a maximized marriage.   ___ True ___ False

11. When something "appreciates," it _____ in value.

Keep this test for your own records.

Lesson 6
Changing Heads

Lesson 6
Changing Heads

A. Change always comes from the _____. *(page 98)*

    1. If change doesn't come from the top, revolution will come from the bottom. *(page 98)*
      ___ True   ___ False

    2. In business, what is always the problem and always the solution? *(circle one) (page 99)*
      money   time   personnel

    3. Read out loud: *"When the righteous are in authority, the people rejoice: but when the wicked beareth rule, the people mourn"* Proverbs 29:2.

    4. Change isn't change, until it's _____. *(page 100)*

B. Intention to change is not change. *(page 100)*

    1. Who must change in the home? *(page 100)*

      _____

For Further Study:

Personnel is the problem and the solution – *"By the blessing of the upright the city is exalted: but it is overthrown by the mouth of the wicked"* Proverbs 11:11.

The solution originates through the man at the top – *"There is an evil which I have seen under the sun, as an error which proceedeth from the ruler"* Ecclesiastes 10:5.

Change – *"And they come to you as people come, and they sit before you as My people, and they hear the words you say, but they will not do them; for with their mouths they show much love, but their hearts go after and are set on their [idolatrous greed for] gain"* Ezekiel 33:31 AMP.

Change begins with you – *"Each of us must bear some faults and burdens of his own. For none of us is perfect"* Galatians 6:5 TLB.

Make changes – *"If you are angry, don't sin by nursing your grudge. Don't let the sun go down with you still angry—get over it quickly. For when you are angry you give a mighty foothold to the devil"* Ephesians 4:26 TLB.

2. Most people judge others by their actions and themselves by their intentions. *(page 100)*

    Name three times recently that you have seen this occur, through personal experience, media or conveyed to you through conversation.

    _____

    _____

    _____

3. Talking about changing, pledging it, making resolutions, considering it—none of these are change. **In your own words**, what would show that change has occurred?

    _____

    _____

C. God says to men: *Let go of all your own ways and depend on _____ in the totality of your _____.* *(page 102)*

For Further Study:

Actions vs. intentions – Parable of the two sons: "'*A man with two sons told the older boy, "Son, go out and work on the farm today." "I won't," he answered, but later he changed his mind and went. Then the father told the youngest, "You go!" and he said, "Yes, sir, I will." But he didn't. Which of the two was obeying his father?' They replied, 'The first, of course.' Then Jesus explained his meaning: 'Surely evil men and prostitutes will get into the Kingdom before you do. For John the Baptist told you to repent and turn to God, and you wouldn't, while very evil men and prostitutes did. And even when you saw this happening, you refused to repent, and so you couldn't believe'*" Matthew 21:28-32 TLB.

Judging others – "*Do not judge, and you will not be judged. Do not condemn, and you will not be condemned. Forgive, and you will be forgiven...For with the measure you use, it will be measured to you...Why do you look at the speck of sawdust in your brother's eye and pay no attention to the plank in your own eye?*" Luke 6:37-38; 41, 42 NIV.

D.   An ounce of obedience is worth a ton of prayer.

   1.   Look up 1 Samuel 15:22. *"Behold, to _____ is better than sacrifice, and to _____ than the fat of rams."*

   2.   Read out loud: *"He that turneth away his ear from hearing the law, even his prayer shall be abomination"* Proverbs 28:9.

   3.   If you don't obey after praying, what happens with your prayers? *(page 104)*

   _____

E.   Change is not change until it's _____. *(page 105)*

   Giving is not giving until it's _____. *(page 105)*

   Faith is not faith until it's _____. *(page 105)*

For Further Study:

Obedience is required – *"Not every one that saith unto me, Lord, Lord, shall enter into the kingdom of heaven; but he that doeth the will of my Father which is in heaven"* Matthew 7:21.

Disobedience nullifies prayers – *"The sacrifice of the wicked is an abomination to the Lord: but the prayer of the upright is his delight"* Proverbs 15:8.

Belief plus action equals faith – *"What good is it...if a man claims to have faith but has no deeds?...For as the body without the spirit is dead, so faith without works is dead also"* James 2:14-26; *"By faith Abraham...offered up Isaac"* Hebrews 11:17-19.

Obedience takes responsibility for failure and exchanges it in prayer for repentance and faith – Psalm 51.

Giving must be given – *"Withhold not good from them to whom it is due, when it is in the power of thine hand to do it. Say not unto thy neighbor, Go, and come again, and tomorrow I will give; when thou hast it by thee"* Proverbs 3:27, 28.

F.   Courage is a requirement of _____. *(page 105)*

1.   Read out loud: *"Be of good courage, and let us play the men for our people, and for the cities of our God: and the Lord do that which seemeth him good"* 2 Samuel 10:12.

In your own words, what is meant by the phrase "play the men"?

_____

2.   *"Be of good _____"* is a scriptural refrain. *(page 105)*

G.   Write out the definition of courage. *(page 106)*

Courage is the _____ that enables

a man to face _____ with a real manliness.

Read out loud: *"Be strong and of a good courage, fear not, nor be afraid of them: for the Lord thy God, he it is that doth go with thee; he will not fail thee, nor forsake thee"* Deuteronomy 31:6.

For Further Study:

It takes courage to be a man – *"Be on your guard; stand firm in the faith; be men of courage; be strong"* 1 Corinthians 16:13 NIV.

Examples of courage – Shadrach, Meshach and Abednego: Daniel 3:16-18; Heroes of the faith: Hebrews 11

Admonished to have courage – *"In the world ye shall have tribulation: but be of good cheer (courage): I have overcome the world"* John 16:33; *"Finally, my brethren, be strong in the Lord, and in the power of his might"* Ephesians 6:10; *"Add to your faith virtue (manliness, courage)"* 2 Peter 1:5.

Leadership requires courage – *"Have I not commanded thee? Be strong and of a good courage; be not afraid, neither be thou dismayed: for the Lord thy God is with thee whithersoever thou goest. Then Joshua commanded the officers and the people"* Joshua 1:9, 10.

H.   Some things in life are more important than _____. *(page 107)*

   1.   Joseph saw the honor of God as the criteria for his life. Read Joseph's statement from Genesis 39:7-9: *"How then can I do this great wickedness, and sin against God?"*

   2.   Name some Biblical heroes who courageously gave their lives for a godly purpose.

   _____

I.   Courage is necessary in a man's life to _____. *(page 107)*

Practical:

1.   A man is seeking God and prays, "God, please help my wife to have a good attitude toward me, and please make my boss recognize what a good job I'm doing." His prayer is admirable, but who is he praying will change? **In your own words**, what would be a better way to pray?

   _____

   _____

For Further Study:

Some things are more important than life itself – *"And they overcame him by the blood of the Lamb, and by the word of their testimony; and they loved not their lives unto the death"* Revelation 12:11; John the Baptist beheaded for speaking the truth: Mark 6:17-27; *"And when he had called the people unto him with his disciples also, he said unto them, Whosoever will come after me, let him deny himself, and take up his cross, and follow me"* Mark 8:34; *"If any man come to me, and hate not his father, and mother, and wife, and children, and brethren, and sisters, yea, and his own life also, he cannot be my disciple"* Luke 14:26.

2. Courage is sometimes necessary to run away from something and sometimes needed to run toward something.

    What do you need courage to run from? _____

    What do you need courage to run toward? _____

3. What can you change in your life today? _____

    How will you go about changing it? _____

    How will you follow up to ensure you've changed? _____

Read this prayer out loud:

Father, in Jesus' Name, I ask You to change me as You have changed so many other men. Help me to accept responsibility for the changes that need to be made and forgive me for blaming others. I will be courageous to change in each area You show me. I will be seen as Your man above all else. Thank You, in Jesus' Name, for walking with me through every step. Amen.

For Further Study:

People must make changes in their hearts, where the problems really are – *"And rend your heart, and not your garments, and turn unto the Lord your God"* Joel 2:13; *"Do not ye yet understand…But those things which proceed out of the mouth come forth from the heart; and they defile the man. For out of the heart proceed evil thoughts, murders, adulteries, fornications, thefts, false witness, blasphemies: These are the things which defile a man"* Matthew 15:17-20.

Heart change – *"Circumcision is that of the heart, in the spirit, and not in the letter"* Romans 2:29; *"A new heart also will I give you, and a new spirit will I put within you: and I will take away the stony heart out of your flesh, and I will give you an heart of flesh"* Ezekiel 36:26; *"Plant the good seeds of righteousness and you will reap a crop of my love; plow the hard ground of your hearts, for now is the time to seek the Lord, that he may come and shower salvation upon you"* Hosea 10:12 TLB; *"Today if you will hear his voice, Harden not your hearts"* Hebrews 3:7-8.

Self-Test *Lesson 6*

1.   If change doesn't come from the top, what will come from the bottom?

   _____

2.   _____ is always the problem; _____ is always the solution.

3.   Men often judge others by their _____ and themselves by their _____.

4.   Give a personal definition of what it means to have courage.

   _____

   _____

   _____

5.   A ton of prayer will always produce more than obedience.   ___ True ___ False

6.   Name the number one virtue that men need in order to face reality. _____

Keep this test for your own records.

Lesson 7

The Buck Stops Here

Lesson 7
The Buck Stops Here

A.   The man is to be the head of the house.

   1.   Read: *"For the husband is the head of the wife as Christ is the head of the church, his body, of which he is the Savior"* Ephesians 5:23 NIV.

   2.   Christ provides _____ to the _____ of the members of the church. The man prayerfully provides _____ to the _____ of his family. *(page 110)*

B.   Men cannot leave the ministry of _____ to their wives. It is their responsibility as well. *(page 115)*

C.   One of the marks of a true leader is not to pass the _____. *(page 115)*

   1.   "Justification" theologically means _____. *(page 115)*

   2.   Self-justification is the term for what we call _____. *(page 115)*

D.   Read Genesis 3:1-10.

   1.   What are the three results of sin? *(page 116)*

   _____   _____   _____

For Further Study:

Solutions to family problems must begin with the father – *"For I know him (Abraham), that he will command his children and his household after him, and they shall keep the way of the Lord"* Genesis 18:19.

Head of the home – *"Husbands, love your wives, even as Christ also loved the church, and gave himself for it; That he might sanctify and cleanse it with the washing of water by the word"* Ephesians 5:25, 26; Ephesians 6:4; Colossians 3:21; 1 Timothy 3:4, 12.

Fathers are blessed when they rear their children in the fear and admonition of the Lord – Deuteronomy 11:18-21.

Fathers are cursed if they neglect their family responsibility – Proverbs 17:25.

Men often try to escape responsibility – Pilate and Jesus: *"Pilate...washed his hands before the multitude, saying, I am innocent of the blood of this just person: see ye to it"* Matthew 27:24.

Self-justification – *"Every way of a man is right in his own eyes: but the Lord pondereth the hearts"* Proverbs 21:2; Luke 16:15.

2. Guilt is a killer. *(page 116)*

Give a Biblical example of someone who was plagued by guilt. _____

3. Guilt leads to _____. *(page 116)*

4. Fear leads to hiding. *(page 116)*

Name some ways in which you have tried to hide or escape from guilt and fear in your life.

_____

_____

E. The devil made you do it!   ___ True ___ False

1. Whom did Adam blame in the Garden of Eden? *(page 116)* _____

2. Whom did Eve blame? *(page 117)* _____

F. Every man must answer to _____ for his own actions. *(page 118)*

1. Some men would rather cover up their _____ than save their marriage. *(page 118)*

2. Others would rather cover up their _____

_____ than save their business. *(page 118)*

For Further Study:

Guilt weighs on a man – *"And they said one to another, We are verily guilty concerning our brother…therefore is this distress come upon us"* Genesis 42:21.

Guilt leads to fear/hiding – *"He said…Intendest thou to kill me, as thou killedst the Egyptian? And Moses feared, and said, Surely this thing is known…Moses fled"* Exodus 2:14, 15; *"Fear hath torment"* 1 John 4:18; *"(The men) hid themselves in the dens and in the rocks of the mountains; And said to the mountains and rocks, Fall on us, and hide us from the face of him that sitteth on the throne, and from the wrath of the Lamb"* Revelation 6:15, 16.

Man must answer to God – *"But why dost thou judge thy brother…for we shall all stand before the judgment seat of Christ"* Romans 14:10.

Sin can be placed and forgiveness received at Calvary – *"How much more shall the blood of Christ, who through the eternal Spirit offered himself without spot to God, purge your conscience from dead works to serve the living God?"* Hebrews 9:14; Colossians 2:13, 14.

Forgiveness requires confession – Psalm 32:5; Proverbs 28:13; James 5:16; 1 John 1:9.

Tragic consequences of covering up mistakes – Achan: Joshua 7:19-26; David and Bathsheba: 2 Samuel 11, 12

G. There are times when silence is golden; other times it is just plain _____. *(page 118)*

H. Some men think they are punishing their child for correction when they are really punishing for

_____. *(page 119)*

The result is that it _____ a child, not changes him. *(page 119)*

I. God is not indifferent to your _____. *(page 122)*

1. God can do nothing for men who say they have no _____. *(page 122)*

2. Read: *"Because thou sayest, I am rich, and increased with goods, and* _____

_____; *and knowest not that thou art wretched, and miserable, and poor, and blind, and naked"* Revelation 3:17.

J. God loves you personally. He has given you _____ and _____. *(page 122)*

To reach your family, God looks to: *(circle one)*

your wife   your church   you

For Further Study:

Men must have spiritual light – *"They know not, neither will they understand; they walk on in darkness: all the foundations of the earth are out of course"* Psalm 82:5; John 1:5; 2 Corinthians 4:4.

Jesus is the Light – *"As long as I am in the world, I am the light of the world"* John 9:5; 2 Corinthians 4:6.

Man revealed by the Light of the Word – *"Thy word is a lamp unto my feet, and a light unto my path"* Psalm 119:105; *"For the commandment is a lamp; and the law is light; and reproofs of instruction are the way of life"* Proverbs 6:23; Hebrews 4:12; 2 Peter 1:19.

God cares about us – Hebrews 2:17, 18; 4:15; Matthew 6:8, 21, 32: 1 Corinthians 10:13.

God can help a man who asks for help – *"Jesus answering said...They that are whole need not a physician; but they that are sick"* Luke 5:31.

God loves you personally – *"The Lord appeared to us in the past, saying: 'I have loved you with an everlasting love; I have drawn you with loving-kindness'"* Jeremiah 31:3; Isaiah 43:1-4; John 3:16.

Live life to the maximum – *"I am come that they might have life, and...have it more abundantly"* John 10:10.

Practical:

1. List on paper all the things you are guilty of or feel guilty about. Spend some time in prayer for God to remind you of sins, mistakes and errors. After writing, mark through each one with red ink as you ask forgiveness for it. As you mark the item, say aloud, "God forgives me, and I now also forgive myself."

2. List the last thing you did that you blamed someone else for. List the one before that, going back as far as you can. Mark through each, using red ink, asking God to forgive you, then forgive yourself. Where appropriate, contact the person you blamed and ask him to forgive you.

What I did

_____

_____

_____

Who I blamed

_____

_____

_____

Repeat this prayer out loud:

Father, in the Name of Jesus, I admit the mistakes and sins that this last lesson has shown me, and I ask for Your forgiveness. Having asked for and received Your forgiveness, I refuse to wallow in self-pity for making them. I refuse to be put down by Satan or others for doing them. I thank You that they are covered with the blood of Jesus and are behind me forever. I accept responsibility for myself, for my situation, for my family and for the way we are today, and I commit to becoming the one who solves the problems, not the one who is part of the problem. For those things I cannot solve, I ask You to cover them with Your grace and mercy and deliver my family and me. I give You praise in advance for a complete change in my life. Amen.

For Further Study:

God has provided a plan for leadership:

Through His Word – *"The words that I speak…they are spirit, and they are life"* John 6:63; *"All Scripture is given by inspiration of God…That the man of God may be perfect… furnished unto all good works"* 2 Timothy 3:16, 17.

Through His Spirit – *"But the Comforter, which is the Holy Ghost, whom the Father will send in my name, he shall teach you all things, and bring all things to your remembrance"* John 14:26; 16:13; Luke 11:13; 1 John 2:27.

Through His wisdom – *"If any of you lack wisdom, let him ask of God"* James 1:5; 1 Corinthians 1:30.

Self-Test *Lesson 7*

1. As the husband, I am responsible to lead the home. Therefore, as Christ takes care of the members of His church, I must _____ for the problems in my home and family.

2. Buck passing is the common term for _____.

3. The sequentially-ordered result of sin is:

    _____

    _____

    _____

4. Name some major ways men try to escape or hide from responsibility.

    _____

    _____

    _____

    _____

5. **In your own words,** write the definition for self-justification.

    _____

    _____

    _____

Keep this test for your own records.

Lesson 8
Video Daddy

Lesson 8
Video Daddy

A.   The most powerful thing that can be done in life is to create an _____; the next most powerful thing is to destroy an _____. *(page 123)*

1.   Men have been victimized by forces and images they could have _____. *(page 124)*

2.   Read: *"But a person whose own heart is evil and untrusting finds evil in everything, for his dirty mind and rebellious heart color all he sees and hears. Such persons claim they know God, but from seeing the way they act, one knows they don't"* Titus 1:15-16 TLB.

Images in our mind influence the way we act, dress, speak…and influence the way we:
*(add more **in your own words**)*

_____   _____   _____

_____   _____   _____

3.   Young men and women are motivated greatly by the _____ they have in life. *(page 126)*

Read: *"For as he thinketh in his heart, so is he"* Proverbs 23:7.
Read: (Spies at the border of Canaan) *"And there we saw the giants…and we were in our own sight as grasshoppers, and so we were in their sight"* Numbers 13:33.

For Further Study:
God created man in His image – Genesis 1:26, 27; God warned against creating images – Leviticus 26:1; God said to destroy images – Numbers 33:52.

Images in our mind motivate our behavior – *"For out of the heart proceed evil thoughts, murders, adulteries, fornications, thefts, false witness, blasphemies"* Matthew 15:19; Romans 1:22-25.

We become the images we have of ourselves – *"Their idols are silver and gold, the work of men's hands…They that make them are like unto them; so is every one that trusteth in them"* Psalm 115:4-8.

We treat others according to our images of them – Treating God like a man: Psalm 50:20, 21.

Degree of disappointment – *"But many of the priests and Levites and chief of the fathers, who were ancient men, that had seen the first house, when the foundation of this house was laid before their eyes, wept with a loud voice; and many shouted aloud for joy"* Ezra 3:12; *"Who is left among you that saw this house in her first glory? And how do ye see it now? Is it not in your eyes in comparison of it as nothing?"* Haggai 2:3.

B. The degree of disappointment is found in the difference between the _____ and the _____. *(page 126)*

C. Without Jesus, men are unable to be restored in the _____. *(page 127)*

When we become new creations, we have new _____. *(page 127)*

D. Form a _____ in your home. *(page 129)*

Read: *"I will make the godly of the land my heroes, and invite them to my home. Only those who are truly good shall be my servants. But I will not allow those who deceive and lie to stay in my house"* Psalm 101:6-7 TLB.

What does this have to do with the "video daddy"? _____
_____
_____

Read: *"And thou shalt teach them diligently unto thy children, and shalt talk of them when thou sittest in thine house, and when thou walkest by the way, and when thou liest down, and when thou risest up"* Deuteronomy 6:7.

What does it mean you should do for your children? _____
_____
_____

For Further Study:

First Adam's image was marred by sin – 1 Corinthians 15:45-49.

Jesus Christ, the second Adam, restored man's image – Romans 8:19; 2 Corinthians 3:18.

Jesus, image of God – *"Who being the brightness of his glory, and the express image of his person"* Hebrews 1:3

Born again through Jesus – *"Not by works of righteousness which we have done, but according to his mercy he saved us, by the washing of regeneration, and renewing of the Holy Ghost"* Titus 3:51; *"Being born again, not of corruptible seed, but of incorruptible, by the word of God, which liveth and abideth for ever"* 1 Peter 1:23.

Without Jesus, man cannot be restored to the image of God – *"For he hath made him to be sin for us, who knew no sin; that we might be made the righteousness of God in him"* 2 Corinthians 5:21; *"For we are his workmanship, created in Christ Jesus unto good works, which God hath before ordained that we should walk in them"* Ephesians 2:10; *"Jesus saith unto him, I am the way, the truth, and the life: no man cometh unto the Father, but by me"* John 14:6.

E.   Man has three functions in the home and community. *(page 129)*

_____   _____   _____

Look up John 17:12; 2 Corinthians 10:4-5; 1 Timothy 3:4.

What points can you learn from these verses? _____

_____

_____

F.   The greatest addiction in today's society is: *(circle one) (page 129)*

drugs   food   alcohol   television   gambling

1.   Read: *"And be not conformed to this world: but be ye transformed by the* _____

of your _____, *that ye may prove what is that good, and acceptable, and perfect, will of God"*
Romans 12:2.

2.   The absentee father in front of the television forces the _____ and _____

into unnatural roles and responsibilities. *(page 129)*

G.   Men, families and nations are made great by the _____ of their virtues, not by virtue of their

_____. *(page 131)*

Men are God's _____. While men look for better _____, God looks

for better _____. *(page 132)*

For Further Study:

Reject wrong spirits and doctrines from your home – *"Submit yourselves therefore to God. Resist the devil, and he will flee from you"* James 4:7; Luke 10:19.

Act like a man – *"Be on your guard; stand firm in the faith; be men of courage; be strong. Do everything in love"* 1 Corinthians 16:13, 14 NIV.

Absentee TV fathers force wives and children into unnatural roles and responsibilities – *"But I suffer not a woman to teach, nor to usurp authority over the man"* 1 Timothy 2:12.

Practical:

1. Start a television log book. HONESTLY keep a record of how much time you spend watching television. Once you've controlled your own television habits, work to control the habits of the rest of the family, making yourself available to fill their time with other activities.

2. Read: *"Watch ye, stand fast in the faith, quit you like men [or act like a man], be strong"* 1 Corinthians 16:13.

    Break it into four parts, and write what you can do to fulfill each one.

    Watch ye: _____

    Stand fast in the faith: _____

    Act like a man: _____

    Be strong: _____

Repeat this prayer out loud:

Father, Your Word says to set no wicked thing before my eyes. This day I make the decision to make a covenant with my eyes, to not look upon images that will grieve Your Spirit and to not glorify the way of evil and violent men. I choose instead to make my home a welcome place for Your Spirit to dwell and abide. I choose to guard well my family whom You have entrusted to my care. In Jesus' Name, Amen.

For Further Study:

Christian TV programming can bring godly people into your home – *"I want the company of the godly men and women in the land; they are the true nobility"* Psalm 16:3 TLB.
Great by wealth of virtue, not by virtue of wealth – *"The good influence of godly citizens causes a city to prosper, but the moral decay of the wicked drives it downhill"* Proverbs 11:11 TLB; *"He that trusteth in his riches shall fall: but the righteous shall flourish as a branch"* Proverbs 11:28; *"Righteousness exalteth a nation: but sin is a reproach to any people"* Proverbs 14:34; *"Take heed, and beware of covetousness: for a man's life consisteth not in the abundance of the things which he possesseth"* Luke 12:15.

Self-Test *Lesson 8*

1. What is the most powerful thing that can be done in a life? _____

2. What is the second most powerful thing that can be done? _____

3. Name some popular "anti-heroes" of today.

    _____

    _____

4. Throughout life, there is a constant adjustment of the _____ and the _____. The distance between the _____ and the _____ is the degree of disappointment in life.

5. Every man has three major functions in the home. What are they?

    _____

    _____

    _____

6. What is the greatest addiction in America today? _____

7. Men are truly great when measured by the wealth of their _____, not the _____ of their wealth.

Keep this test for your own records.

Lesson 9
Our Father, Which Art Inactive
&
Stop, Look, Listen

Lesson 9

Our Father, Which Art Inactive & Stop, Look, Listen

I.   Our Father, Which Art Inactive (Chapter 12)

  A.   The greatest thing a father can do for his children is _____ their mother. *(page 133)*

   1.   Read: *"Husbands, love your wives and do not be harsh with them"* Colossians 3:19 NIV.
   2.   Read: *"Do nothing out of selfish ambition or vain conceit, but in humility consider others better than yourselves. Each of you should look not only to your own interests, but also to the interests of others. Your attitude should be the same as that of Christ Jesus"* Philippians 2:3-5 NIV.

       What attitudes and attributes from these verses might God expect in a husband?

       _____

  B.   Fathering is a comprehensive task requiring maximized manhood.

   1.   Fathering takes: *(page 136)* *(fill in more requirements, **in your own words**)*
       thinking   studying   monitoring   recommending   influencing   loving

       _____   _____   _____

       _____   _____   _____

   2.   Read: *"Work hard so God can say to you, 'Well done.' Be a good workman, one who does not need to be ashamed when God examines your work"* 2 Timothy 2:15 TLB.

       What does this mean to you?   _____

       _____

For Further Study:

Instruction to married men – *"Live joyfully with the wife whom thou lovest all the days of the life of thy vanity"* Ecclesiastes 9:9; *"Husbands, in the same way be considerate as you live with your wives, and treat them with respect as the weaker partner and as heirs with you of the gracious gift of life, so that nothing will hinder your prayers"* 1 Peter 3:7 NIV. Give your family a gesture of love today – *"Now I want you to be leaders also in the spirit of cheerful giving...This is one way to prove your love is real, that it goes beyond mere words"* 2 Corinthians 8:7, 8 TLB; *"Let us not love in word, neither in tongue; but in deed and in truth"* 1 John 3:18. Children blessed by fathers – *"Blessed is the man who fears the Lord, who finds great delight in his commands. His children will be mighty in the land; the generation of the upright will be blessed"* Psalm 112:1, 2 NIV; *"The just man walketh in his integrity: his children are blessed after him"* Proverbs 20:7.

C.   Love is doing what is best for the one _____, not gratifying our own desires at the expense of _____. *(page 136)*

D.   What hour is one of the most important in a child's life? *(circle one) (pages 136–137)*

      show and tell   naptime   dinner time   Sesame Street

E.   Television

    1.   Look up John 10:10. *"The thief cometh not, but for to _____, and to kill, and to destroy."*

    2.   One of the greatest thieves of family time is _____. *(page 137)*

    3.   Uncontrolled, television time will: *(page 137)*
        a. _____ time   b. kill _____   c. _____ relationships

    4.   Read out loud:
        "Hard work means prosperity; only a fool idles away his time" Proverbs 12:11 TLB.
        "Reverence for God adds hours to each day" Proverbs 10:27 TLB.

        How can you apply these verses to yourself? _____

        _____

For Further Study:

The family meal – *"You must teach them (the Lord's commandments) to your children and talk about them when you are at home or out for a walk; at bedtime and the first thing in the morning"* Deuteronomy 6:7; *"Your wife shall be contented in your home. And look at all those children! There they sit around the dinner table as vigorous and healthy as young olive trees. That is God's reward to those who reverence and trust him"* Psalm 128:3, 4 TLB; *"When our sons shall be as plants grown large in their youth and our daughters as sculptured corner pillars hewn like those of a palace"* Psalm 144:12 AMP; Acts 2:46.

Unproductive time – *"He also that is slothful in his work is brother to him that is a great waster"* Proverbs 18:9; *"By much slothfulness the building decayeth; and through idleness of the hands the house droppeth through"* Ecclesiastes 10:18.

Leading the family in righteousness – *"For I know him (Abraham), that he will command his children and his household after him, and they shall keep the way of the Lord"* Genesis 18:19.

A man of God leads his family in truth by keeping his word – Proverbs 11:3.

F.   The _____ father is the curse of our day. *(page 138)*
Think it over: The average American father gives only *thirty-five seconds* of undivided attention to his child every day. *"A child left to himself bringeth his mother to shame"* Proverbs 29:15.

G.   The true legacy of the father is in the _____ he gives his children. *(page 139)*
"A good man leaveth an inheritance to his _____*"* Proverbs 13:22.

H.   _____ funds can never be a substitute for a _____ of _____. *(page 139)*

I .   The children of a maximized man will be taught a strong relationship with God. *(page 139)*
___ True ___ False

II.   Stop, Look, Listen (Chapter 13)

A.   The one who _____ before he _____ will succeed. *(page 141)*

B.   Read: *"He who answers before listening—that is his folly and his shame"* Proverbs 18:13 NIV.
"Wherefore, my beloved brethren, let every man be swift to hear, slow to speak, slow to wrath" James 1:19.
"He that hath an ear, let him hear what the Spirit saith" Revelation 2:7.

1.   God's attitude is that success is a result of _____. *(page 141)*

2.   To succeed in sales or counseling, listen until you hear what the _____ is, then meet it. *(page 141)*

3.   Listening is _____. *(page 141)*

4.   What priority does God place on listening? *(page 141)*

_____

For Further Study:

Good men leave an inheritance – *"For the children ought not to lay up for the parents, but the parents for the children"* 2 Corinthians 12:14.
The family of a man of God can depend on him – *"A faithful man shall abound with blessings"* Proverbs 28:20.
Maximized families – *"And ye shall teach them (God's Words) your children...That your days may be multiplied, and the days of your children, in the land which the Lord sware unto your fathers to give them, as the days of heaven upon the earth"* Deuteronomy 11:19-21; *"The father of the righteous shall greatly rejoice: and he that begetteth a wise child shall have joy of him"* Proverbs 23:24.
Importance of listening – *"The Lord...called...Samuel answered, Speak; for thy servant heareth"* 1 Samuel 3:10; *"Guard your steps when you go to the house of God. Go near to listen rather than to offer the sacrifice of fools, who do not know that they do wrong"* Ecclesiastes 5:1.

5. Men must learn to _____. *(page 142)*

C. Men and women are different!

   1. Men need to learn to listen to their wives and children: *(check all that apply) (page 142)*

     ____ to affirm their uniqueness   ____ to learn their needs

     ____ to discover if they are satisfied   ____ to keep the relationship solid

     ____ to make the relationship grow   ____ to hear their inner longings

   2. Men are _____. Women are _____ people. *(page 143)*

   3. The fine print is part of _____. To minister to a woman, you must

     give her some _____. *(page 144)*

D. The sin of _____ is the basic sin of humanity. *(page 144)*

   1. The only reason you do _____ is because you don't do right. *(page 144)*

   2. Men go to Hell not because of what they _____ but because of what they _____.
     (page 144)

   3. To begin doing right, we must fill our minds with godly _____ and divine _____.
     (page 145)

   4. Read: *"Therefore to him that knoweth to do _____, and doeth it not, to him it is _____"*
     James 4:17.

For Further Study:

Be a counselor by way of listening – *"Whosoever will be great among you, let him be your minister: And whosoever will be chief among you, let him be your servant: Even as the Son of man came not to be ministered unto, but to minister"* Matthew 20:26-28; *"Husbands, love your wives, even as Christ also loved the church, and gave himself for it"* Ephesians 5:25; *"You husbands must be careful of your wives, being thoughtful of their needs and honoring them as the weaker sex"* 1 Peter 3:7 TLB.

The most fatal sin of omission is not believing on Jesus – John 3:16-19, 36.

Fill minds with godly thoughts – *"When they knew God, they glorified him not as God, neither were thankful; but became vain in their imaginations, and their foolish heart was darkened"* Romans 1:21; *"And the peace of God, which transcends all understanding, will guard your hearts and your minds in Christ Jesus…Brothers, whatever is true, whatever is noble, whatever is right, whatever is pure, whatever is lovely, whatever is admirable—if anything is excellent or praiseworthy—think about such things. Whatever you have learned or received or heard from me, or seen in me—put it into practice. And the God of peace will be with you"* Philippians 4:7-9 NIV.

E. Communication is the _____ of life. *(page 145)*

Read: *"It is written, That man shall not live by bread alone, but by every word of God"* Luke 4:4.

How important is God's Word to us? _____

How important should our word to others be? _____

Practical:

1. Commit to spend a "private time" weekly or monthly with every member of your family just to LISTEN. Your family doesn't need to know your intentions. Just follow your plan, and they'll eventually figure out what you're doing. Ask them leading questions to draw them out. Save your comments until later. If they are negative in your first few "private times," remember that you are making an investment, and both consistent listening and prayer will help re-establish relationship.

    "Private time" with my wife   Time/Day: _____

    "Private time" with my child   Time/Day: _____

    "Private time" with my child   Time/Day: _____

    "Private time" with my child   Time/Day: _____

2. A father sees his toddler hit a household table with a toy, marring it. He yells and grabs the toy from the child, swatting the child and scolding him, ordering him out of the room.

    Is he punishing or correcting the child? _____

    What is another way he could handle the situation? _____

    _____

For Further Study:

Discipline is necessary – *"He will die for lack of discipline and instruction"* Proverbs 5:23 AMP; Proverbs 22:6, 15; 23:13, 14 AMP; Hebrews 12:10, 11.
Proper correction – *"And ye fathers, provoke not your children to wrath: but nurture them in the chastening and admonition of the Lord"* Ephesians 6:4; *"Not domineering [as arrogant, dictatorial, and overbearing persons] over those in your charge, but being examples (patterns and models of Christian living)"* 1 Peter 5:3 AMP.
Discipline must be done in love – *"He who spares his rod [of discipline] hates his son, but he who loves him disciplines diligently and punished him early"* Proverbs 13:24; Hebrews 12:5-7; *"Discipline your son while there is hope, but do not [indulge your angry resentments by undue chastisements and] set yourself to his ruin"* Proverbs 19:18 AMP.

3. The fourteen-year-old son stays in his room, listening to music and playing on his computer. The parents worry, but the father insists they must respect the boy's privacy.

Is he giving the boy freedom or losing his relationship with him? _____

What might he do differently to reach out to his son? _____

_____

4. Set a date on your calendar three weeks from now. Every day for the next three weeks, concentrate on listening to people until they are finished, not worrying about what you'll say next.

5. Often men don't even listen to a name that's given. When you know you'll be introduced to someone, plan ahead to listen carefully to the name, and immediately repeat it several times to commit it to memory.

6. In what areas of your life are you failing because of what you are NOT doing?

_____

Repeat this prayer out loud:

Father, in Jesus' Name, I want to be a quality listener. I choose today to walk in love and be patient as I listen to my wife and children. I will incline my ear to You and to my family and search to understand what they are really wanting to communicate to me. Forgive me for my impatience toward them. Thank You for Your patience toward me. Once again I ask for Your forgiveness—this time for my sins of omission, as well as my sins of commission. Please cleanse me from unrighteousness, purify my mind through Your Word, and bring me ever more into the newness of life Your Son provides for me. I confess the power of Christ within me to overcome old habits, restore right relationships and keep me on the straight course I have chosen. Thank You for making the way for me. I love you, Lord. Amen.

For Further Study:

Results of godly discipline – *"The rod and reproof give wisdom: but a child left to himself bringeth his mother to shame; Correct thy son, and he shall give thee rest; yea, he shall give delight unto thy soul"* Proverbs 29:15, 17; *"All Scripture is given by inspiration of God, and is profitable for doctrine, for reproof, for correction, for instruction in righteousness: That the man of God may be perfect, thoroughly furnished unto all good works"* 2 Timothy 3:16-17.

Self-Test *Lesson 9*

1. The greatest thing a man can do for his children is: *(circle one)*

    love their mother   correct them   give them gifts

2. What is one of the major curses of the day? _____

3. Name three attributes God expects in a good husband and father.

    _____

    _____

    _____

4. Name three activities God expects in a good husband and father.

    _____

    _____

    _____

5. _____ desires to benefit others even at the expense of self, because _____ desires to give.

6. What thief affects families in America today? _____

7. Men are head-liners; women are _____ people.

8. What is the basic sin of humanity? _____

9. a. _____ is the basis of life.

    b. When communication stops, _____ sets in.

    c. The ultimate end of abnormality is _____.

10. Men must stop and listen to their family's _____.

Keep this test for your own records.

Lesson 10

Born-Again Marriage
&
What's the Question?

Lesson 10
Born-Again Marriage & What's the Question?

I. Born-Again Marriage (Chapter 14)
A. Marriages are ordained by God.

    1. Read out loud: *"For this reason a man will leave his father and mother and be united to his wife, and the two will become one flesh"* Ephesians 5:31 NIV.

    2. Marriage can be the closest thing to a _____ or a _____ on this earth. *(page 148)*

B. Jesus is the Savior of every area of our lives.

    1. It is harder to _____ than it is to _____. *(page 151)*

    2. Read: *"And these are they likewise which are sown on stony ground; who, when they have heard the word, immediately receive it with gladness; And have no root in themselves, and so endure but for a time"* Mark 4:16-17.

    What areas of your life are difficult to maintain? *(check any that apply)*

    ____ love in marriage   ____ patience with children   ____ positive attitude

    ____ weight loss   ____ enthusiasm for work   ____ prayer life

    other _____

For Further Study:

God ordained marriage – *"This explains why a man leaves his father and mother and is joined to his wife in such a way that the two become one person"* Genesis 2:24 TLB; *"'The Creator "made them male and female," and said, "For this reason a man will leave his father and mother and be united to his wife, and the two will become one flesh"? So they are no longer two, but one. Therefore what God has joined together, let man not separate'"* Matthew 19:4-6; *"Honor your marriage and its vows, and be pure; for God will surely punish all those who are immoral or commit adultery"* Hebrews 13:4 TLB.

Hurts and misunderstandings can develop prior to or early in marriage – Jacob and Leah: Genesis 29:21-35.

A man of God gives his word in marriage and keeps it, no matter how difficult – *"Therefore guard your passions! Keep faith with the wife of your youth. For the Lord, the God of Israel, says he hates divorce and cruel men. Therefore control your passions—let there be no divorcing of your wives"* Malachi 2:15-16 TLB.

Christ reproduced His life within us – *"And I will pray the Father, and he shall give you another Comforter, that he may abide with you for ever"* John 14:16, 17.

3. Jesus gives us life principles and _____ to live according to those principles. *(page 151)*

4. Jesus is the Savior of your _____. *(page 151)*

5. Jesus has a place in marriage and family in the same way He has with an individual.

    Read: *"And one standing alone can be attacked and defeated, but two can stand back-to-back and conquer; three is even better, for a triple-braided cord is not easily broken"* Ecclesiastes 4:12 TLB.

    How does this verse apply to your marriage? _____
    _____

II. What's the Question? (Chapter 15)

    A. One major reason for so much _____ today is because of so little _____. *(page 156)*

    When people spend time in _____, meditating in it, praying over it, confessing it, it will become their counselor. *(page 156)*

    B. Men have two great questions to answer in life. *(page 158) (Luke 9:18-20)*

    1. _____   2. _____

    C. Manhood is like a magic art. *(page 159)*   ___ True ___ False

---

For Further Study:

Jesus saves every area of your life, providing enabling power to live according to His principles – *"I am come that they might have life, and that they might have it more abundantly"* John 10:10; *"But as many as received him, to them gave he power to become the sons of God, even to them that believe on his name"* John 1:12; *"But ye shall receive power, after that the Holy Ghost is come upon you"* Acts 1:8.

Jesus has a place in marriage – *"What God has joined together, let man not separate"* Mark 10:7 NIV.

Prayer produces intimacy – *"They joined with the other believers in regular attendance at...prayer meetings...And all the believers...shared everything with each other"* Acts 2:42-44 TLB.

God desires intimacy which leads to friendship with Him – John 17:21; *"Friendship with God is reserved for those who reverence him. With them alone he shares the secrets of his promises"* Psalm 25:14 TLB; *"He gives his friendship to the godly"* Proverbs 3:32 TLB.

Prayer requires honesty with God – *"The Lord is nigh unto all them that call upon him...in truth"* Psalm 145:18; *"Call unto me, and I will answer thee, and show thee great and mighty things, which thou knowest not"* Jeremiah 33:3; Philippians 4:6.

D.   Abraham pitched his _____ but built his _____. *(page 159)*

    1.   Today many men spend too much time on the _____ and not enough on the _____. *(page 159)*

    Read: *"Since, then, you have been raised with Christ, set your hearts on things above, where Christ is seated at the right hand of God. Set your minds on things above, not on earthly things"* Colossians 3:1-2 NIV.

    2.   You can pitch _____, but you must build _____. *(page 159)*

    Read: *"Charm can be deceptive and beauty doesn't last"* Proverbs 31:30 TLB.

    3.   When the _____ wears off, you have nothing but _____ left. *(page 159)*

E.   Churches, homes and nations are only as strong as their men.

    1.   To be strong, man must conquer _____. *(page 160)*

    Read: *"It is better to be slow-tempered than famous; it is better to have self-control than to control an army"* Proverbs 16:32 TLB.

    Read: *"A man without self-control is as defenseless as a city with broken-down walls"* Proverbs 25:28 TLB.

For Further Study:

Lay a right foundation for your character – 2 Corinthians 7:1; Proverbs 21:8; 24:3, 4; 31:23, 30, 31 AMP.

A man's word and character – *"A good man out of the good treasure of his heart bringeth forth that which is good…for of the abundance of the heart his mouth speaketh"* Luke 6:45.

Personality is not the same as character – 1 Samuel 16:7; Proverbs 26:23.

He who honors God privately will show good character in decisions – Psalm 119:101, 102, 104; Proverbs 14:2.

Strong men are required for success – *"The good influence of godly citizens causes a city to prosper, but the moral decay of the wicked drives it downhill"* Proverbs 11:11 TLB; *"Moreover it is required in stewards, that a man be found faithful"* 1 Corinthians 4:2; *"Without wise leadership, a nation is in trouble"* Proverbs 11:14 TLB; Matthew 7:15-16; *"With good men in authority, the people rejoice; but with the wicked in power, they groan"* Proverbs 29:2 TLB; *"When there is moral rot within a nation, its government topples easily"* Proverbs 28:2 TLB.

2. Manhood and _____ are synonymous. *(page 160)*

Read: *"For from the very beginning God decided that those who came to him—and all along he knew who would—should become like his Son, so that his Son would be the First, with many brothers"* Romans 8:29 TLB.

What does this mean to you personally? _____

_____

Practical:

1. Manhood is not magic but rather a building process. What areas can you begin to "press through" in your quest for manhood? _____

2. Read: *"Bodily exercise is all right, but spiritual exercise is much more important and is a tonic for all you do. So exercise yourself spiritually and practice being a better Christian, because that will help you not only now in this life, but in the next life too"* 1 Timothy 4:8 TLB.
   What will you do to "exercise" yourself spiritually and start the Christ-life in you?

   _____

   _____

Repeat this prayer out loud:

Father, in Jesus' Name, I have made my decision—no more wavering, no more hesitating. I will become the man You created me to be, the man You've always seen I could be. I have Your faith operating in me and the power of Your Son making me like Him. I will do the work of being a man, a husband, a father, and I will show myself to be a worthy son of Yours. Thank You for loving me, strengthening me and covering me with the blood of Christ. Amen.

For Further Study:

Maturation is a lifelong process – *"Be perfect [growing into complete maturity of godliness in mind and character, having reached the proper height of virtue and integrity], as your heavenly Father is perfect"* Matthew 10:48 AMP; *"Suffering produces perseverance; perseverance, character; and character, hope"* Romans 5:3-5 NIV; Galatians 6:9.
Character is built in private, developed from a lifetime of individual decisions that enhance or diminish it – *"I have chosen the way of truth: thy judgments have I laid before me"* Psalm 119:30; *"If a man…purge himself from these, he shall be a vessel unto honour, sanctified, and meet for the master's use, and prepared unto every good work"* 2 Timothy 2:21.
God commits to character, not talent – *"And the things you have heard me say in the presence of many witnesses entrust to reliable men who will also be qualified to teach others"* 2 Timothy 2:2; Matthew 25:21; Luke 16:10.

Self-Test *Lesson 10*

1. What is possibly the closest thing to a heaven or a hell that an individual will ever experience on earth?

    _____

2. Which is more difficult—maintaining or obtaining?

    _____

3. Jesus gives us _____ to live by, and His _____
    to do it.

4. Abraham pitched his altars but built his tents.   ___ True   ___ False

5. Men pitch personality, but _____ must be built.

6. _____ and _____ are synonymous.

Keep this test for your own records.

Lesson 11
Adult Boys & It's the Heart

Lesson 11
Adult Boys & It's the Heart

I.   Adult Boys (Chapter 16)
    A.   The curse of our day is _____. Rather than being absent from the family, there is an absence of _____ for the family. *(page 161)*

    B.   You are young only once, but you can live immature for a lifetime. *(page 162)* ___ True ___ False

        1.   Use the following words to fill in the blanks below: *(page 162)*

           child   childishness   mother   childlikeness

           God commends _____ but scorns _____.

           When a man acts like a _____, it forces his wife to act like his _____.

        2.   Name a common feature of childishness in a man today. _____ _____ *(page 162)*

           What is the fallacy of pornography? *(page 162)* _____ _____

           While promising _____, pornography provides it only with himself. *(page 162)*

           Pornography is actually _____. *(page 163)*

For Further Study:

Fathers are blessed if they rear their children in the fear and admonition of the Lord – Deuteronomy 11:18-21.
Fathers are cursed if they neglect their family responsibility – *"Set an example…in speech, in life, in love, in faith and in purity"* 1 Timothy 4:11-13 NIV; Proverbs 17:25; Titus 2:2-8.
Don't live immature – *"When I became a man, I put away childish things"* 1 Corinthians 13:11.
Idolatrous fantasizing and private sex sins are a sin against one's own manhood – Deuteronomy 7:26.
Pornography deceives and dominates – *"Jesus answered them, Verily, verily, I say unto you, Whosoever committeth sin is the servant of sin"* John 8:34; *"While they promise them liberty, they themselves are the servants of corruption: for of whom a man is overcome, of the same is he brought in bondage"* 2 Peter 2:19.
Do not be idolaters – *"I made a covenant with my eyes not to look lustfully at a girl"* Job 31:1 NIV; *"I will set before my eyes no vile thing. The deeds of faithless men I hate; they will not cling to me"* 1 Corinthians 10:6-11 NIV; 2 Timothy 2:19.

3. Use the following words to fill in the blanks below: *(page 163)*

idolatry   place   mind

The "high places" of the _____ are compared to the high places of _____ that the nation of Israel created to take the _____ of worship to Jehovah God.

C. Maturity doesn't come with age but begins with the acceptance of: *(circle one)* *(page 163)*

leadership   a position   responsibility

1. What is a major difference between the First Adam and the Last Adam? *(page 163)*

_____

_____

_____

2. Compare immature, childish men with mature, Christlike men of covenant. *(page 163)*

Immature, childish men	Christlike men of covenant

For Further Study:

Pornography creates a stronghold in the mind, a snare to the life – Psalm 106:36.

Maturity accepts responsibility – *"David was the youngest: and the three eldest followed Saul. And David said to Saul, Let no man's heart fail because of him; thy servant will go and fight with this Philistine"* 1 Samuel 17:14, 32; *"Preach the word; be instant in season, out of season"* 2 Timothy 4:2.

First Adam blames others – *"The woman whom thou gavest…me, she gave me of the tree, and I did eat"* Genesis 3:12; *"A man may ruin his chances by his own foolishness and then blame it on the Lord!"* Proverbs 19:3 TLB.

Accepting responsibility for the actions of others contributes to your own greatness – *"Let this mind be in you, which was also in Christ Jesus: Who, being in the form of God, thought it not robbery to be equal with God: But made himself of no reputation and took upon him the form of a servant, and was made in the likeness of men: And being found in fashion as a man, he humbled himself, and became obedient unto death, even the death of the cross"* Philippians 2:5-8; David was made king: Acts 13:22.

A man's ways – Proverbs 16:2; 21:2

3. According to the book, name a man's three options. *(page 163)*

To be _____

To be _____

To be _____

D. What did Jesus tell the religious men was their reason for rejecting Him and John the Baptist before Him? *(pages 164–165)* _____

_____

1. The "religious" men were childish and petty, and they insisted others live by their philosophy. This was actually what? *(page 165)* _____

_____

What is the result of men living by someone else's philosophy? *(page 165)* _____

_____

2. Is being able to overcome failure a measure of mature manhood? *(page 165)* ___ Yes ___ No

E. Availability is not the greatest need in business or ministry; _____ is. *(circle one)* *(page 165)*

education   teachability   a proven track record

For Further Study:

Don't live by another's philosophy – *"Blessed is the man that walketh not in the counsel of the ungodly, nor standeth in the way of sinners, nor sitteth in the seat of the scornful"* Psalm 1:1; Don't "mingle seed" – Leviticus 19:19; Ezra 9:2.

Self-justification – *"Every way of a man is right in his own eyes: but the Lord pondereth the hearts"* Proverbs 21:2.

Overcome failure – *"Now I rejoice, not that ye were made sorry, but that ye sorrowed to repentance…For godly sorrow worketh repentance to salvation"* 2 Corinthians 7:9-10; *"Not as though I had already attained, either were already perfect: but I follow after, if that I may apprehend that for which also I am apprehended of Christ Jesus"* Philippians 3:12.

God has no plan for failure but He does for failures – *"I am come that they might have life, and that they might have it more abundantly"* John 10:10.

Winners are not those who never fail but those who never quit – 1 Corinthians 16:13.

Teachability – *"My son, if thou wilt receive my words, and hide my commandments with thee…Then shalt thou understand the fear of the Lord, and find the knowledge of God"* Proverbs 2:1, 5; 3:13, 16, 17; Proverbs 12:1 TLB.

II. It's the Heart (Chapter 17)

    A. Use the following words to fill in the blanks: *(page 168)*

       present   past   future

       "You sow to the _____ but reap from the _____."

      1. The mind comes before the heart in telling us about our bodies and our lives. It is the mind we should listen to more than our heart. *(page 169)* ___ True ___ False

      2. Read aloud the following scriptures:
         "Keep your heart with all diligence, for out of it are the issues of life" Proverbs 4:23.
         "For as he thinketh in his heart, so is he" Proverbs 23:7.

      3. It is from the _____, not from the _____, that good and evil come forth. It is why God made it possible for us through faith in Christ to be "born again" and to have a new _____, a _____ that receives and contains the Spirit of God and brings forth the good things of Christ. *(page 170)*

For Further Study:

Sowing and reaping – *"They that sow in tears shall reap in joy"* Psalm 126:5; *"The sluggard will not plow by reason of the cold; therefore shall he beg in harvest, and have nothing"* Proverbs 20:4; *"He that observeth the wind shall not sow; and he that regardeth the clouds shall not reap"* Ecclesiastes 11:4; *"If you wait for perfect conditions, you will never get anything done"* Ecclesiastes 11:4 TLB.

It's the heart – *"I have inclined mine heart to perform thy statutes always, even unto the end"* Psalm 119:112; *"My son, forget not my law; but let thine heart keep my commandments: For length of days, and long life, and peace, shall they add to thee"* Proverbs 3:1-2; *"And let the peace (soul harmony which comes) from Christ rule (act as umpire continually) in your hearts [deciding and settling with finality all questions that arise in your minds, in that peaceful state]"* Colossians 3:15 AMP; *"Draw nigh to God, and he will draw nigh to you. Cleanse your hands, ye sinners; and purify your hearts, ye double minded"* James 4:8.

4. Read aloud: *"Jesus said unto him, Thou shalt love the Lord thy God with all thy heart, and with all thy soul, and with all your mind. This is the first and great commandment. And the second is like unto it, Thou shalt love thy neighbour as thyself"* Matthew 22:37-39.

   What does God say should come first? *(page 171)* _____

5. Write Isaiah 29:13. _____

   _____

   _____

6. Loving God must _____, _____

   and be _____ the heart. *(page 171)*

7. The heart that has become new in Christ is: *(page 171)*
   a. _____ God's Word   b. _____ God's Word
   c. _____ to God's Word.

B. What must you do to love God? *(page 172)*

   _____

   Marriage is a _____, even as salvation is a _____ made with us

   through the shedding of Christ's blood on the Cross. A _____ is more than a contract.

   It's all a matter of the _____. *(page 172)*

For Further Study:

A changed heart – *"Give therefore thy servant an understanding heart...that I may discern between good and bad"* 1 Kings 3:9; *"A real Jew is anyone whose heart is right with God. For God is...looking for those with changed hearts and minds. Whoever has that kind of change in his life will get his praise from God"* Romans 2:29 TLB; *"But sanctify the Lord God in your hearts"* 1 Peter 3:15.

What's in the heart – *"With my whole heart have I sought thee: O let me not wander from thy commandments. Thy word have I hid in mine heart, that I might not sin against thee...Deal bountifully with thy servant, that I may live, and keep thy word"* Psalm 119:10-11, 17; *"Let thine heart retain my words: keep my commandments, and live"* Proverbs 4:4; *"Keep my commandments, and live; and my law as the apple of thine eye. Bind them upon thy fingers, write them upon the table of thine heart"* Proverbs 7:2-3; *"A good man out of the good treasure of his heart bringeth forth that which is good...for of the abundance of the heart his mouth speaketh"* Luke 6:45.

Christ gave His blood for our *"eternal redemption"* and is *"the mediator of a new covenant"* – Hebrews 9:12, 15 NIV.

Practical:

1. What is the purpose of the five-fold ministry gifts in the church? *(page 162)*

    _____

    _____

2. Declining morality follows declining love for God. Give an example of this.

    _____

    _____

3. God knows our hearts and made it possible for us to have new hearts. List at least three things that come

    out of a new heart. *(pages 172–173)* _____

    _____

    Are the ones you listed showing or lacking in your life?

Pray this prayer out loud:

Father, I ask You to help me be a father who is concerned for his family. Let me be mature and responsible in all my actions and thoughts. I want to have a pure mind that desires to worship You. Let me choose to be a Christlike covenant man who accepts responsibility for myself, for my family and for the world. Help me to be teachable and to live by Your Word and not by the philosophies of others. Show me how to listen to my heart, and let my heart be sensitive to Your voice. I choose to love what You love and to hate what You hate. May my love for You never wane. Amen.

For Further Study:

Grow up into the stature of the measure of being Christlike –
Men are accountable for six areas of responsibility, based on 1 Timothy 3:1-11 – Reputation: 1 Thessalonians 5:22; 2 Corinthians 6:3; Ethics: 1 Timothy 4:16; Morality and Temperament: 2 Timothy 2:24, 25; Habits: 1 Timothy 4:8; Maturity: 1 Timothy 4:15.
"Out of the abundance of the heart the mouth speaketh" Matthew 12:34.
"Create in me a clean heart, O God; and renew a right spirit within me. Cast me not away from thy presence; and take not thy holy spirit from me. Restore unto me the joy of thy salvation; and uphold me with thy free spirit. Then will I teach transgressors thy ways; and sinners shall be converted unto thee" Psalm 51:10-13.
"The righteous shall move onward and forward; those with pure hearts shall become stronger and stronger" Job 17:9 TLB.
"Delight thyself also in the Lord; and he shall give thee the desires of thine heart. Commit thy way unto the Lord; trust also in him; and he shall bring it to pass" Psalm 37:4-5.

Self-Test *Lesson 11*

1. The curse of our day is _____. Rather than being absent from the family, there is an absence of _____ for the family.

2. Name a common feature of childishness in a man today. _____
    _____.

3. Maturity doesn't come with age but begins with the acceptance of: *(circle one)*

    leadership   a position   responsibility

4. Name a man's three options.

    To be _____

    To be _____

    To be _____

5. Availability is not the greatest need in business or ministry, _____ is. *(circle one)*

    education   teachability   a proven track record

6. The heart comes before the mind in telling us about our bodies and our lives. It is our heart more than our mind we should listen to.   ___ True   ___ False

7. In Matthew 22:37-39, what does God say should come first? _____

8. Loving God must _____, _____ and be
    _____ the heart.

9. What must you do to love God? _____
    _____

10. Marriage is a _____, even as salvation is a _____ made with us
    through the shedding of Christ's blood on the Cross. A _____ is more than a contract.
    It's all a matter of the _____.

Keep this test for your own records.

Lesson 12
Take It to the Cross!
&
That's My Dad!
&
Burn Out, Don't Fade Out

Lesson 12

Take It to the Cross! & That's My Dad! & Burn Out, Don't Fade Out

I.   Take It to the Cross! (Chapter 18)
   A.   Use the following words to fill in the blanks: *(page 174)*

   change   life   maturity   problems

   1.   The only constant in _____ is _____. How you handle _____ shows your level of _____.

   2.   Redemption for man was accomplished on _____. *(page 174)*

   3.   _____ is the culminating place of worship. _____ is the place of exchange. When you go to _____, you leave different from the way you came. *(page 175)*

   4.   "Take it to the cross" is the title and banner under which eternal change takes place in our lives. Write the letter that completes the phrase. *(page 175)* We take to the Cross:

____ Guilt	and leave with	a. acceptance
____ Repentance	and leave with	b. righteousness
____ Sorrow	and leave with	c. healing
____ Sin	and leave with	d. acquittal
____ Stupidity	and leave with	e. power
____ Ignorance	and leave with	f. faith
____ Disease	and leave with	g. wisdom
____ Rejection	and leave with	h. joy
____ Impotence	and leave with	i. eternal knowledge

For Further Study:

Jesus said, *"Greater love hath no man than this, that a man lay down his life for his friends"* John 15:13. Then He proved it by laying down His life for us on Calvary's Cross. *"To him that overcometh will I grant to sit with me in my throne, even as I also overcame, and am set down with my Father in his throne"* Revelation 3:21.

Deliverance to salvation requires deliverance from sin – *"Her sins, which are many, are forgiven; for she loved much: but to whom little is forgiven, the same loveth little"* Luke 7:47; *"For he hath made him to be sin for us, who knew no sin; that we might be made the righteousness of God in him"* 2 Corinthians 5:21.

Make changes, be renewed – *"When I became a man, I put away childish things"* 1 Corinthians 13:11; *"Put off... the old man, which is corrupt according to the deceitful lusts; And be renewed in the spirit of your mind; And that ye put on the new man, which after God is created in righteousness and true holiness"* Ephesians 4:22-24.

5. How did God display His love for the world? *(page 175)* _____

6. The Cross is where God's wrath against _____ was appeased by Christ's sacrifice. *(circle one)* *(page 176)*

    man   sin   Satan

B. None of us can live according to the law, because we are lawbreakers by nature. *(page 176)*

    ___ True ___ False

1. The law shows us we are sin-sick by nature. We are in need of a cure. What is the cure?
(page 176) _____

2. What is the devil's lie? *(page 177)* _____
_____

C. To omit the Cross is to make _____ just like any other religion. *(page 178)*

1. Check "Yes" or "No" for the following statements about the Cross. *(pages 178–179)*
    ___ Yes ___ No   Jesus triumphed over principalities and powers.
    ___ Yes ___ No   Satan's power was increased.
    ___ Yes ___ No   We are crucified to the world.
    ___ Yes ___ No   The world is crucified to us.

2. Explain the difference between His Cross and our cross. *(page 179)*
_____
_____

For Further Study:

God displayed His love for us – *"Let this mind be in you, which was also in Christ Jesus: Who, being in the form of God, thought it not robbery to be equal with God: But made himself of no reputation and took upon him the form of a servant, and was made in the likeness of men: And being found in fashion as a man, he humbled himself, and became obedient unto death, even the death of the cross"* Philippians 2:5-8; *"Who being the brightness of his glory, and the express image of his person, and upholding all things by the word of his power, when he had by himself purged our sins, sat down on the right hand of the Majesty on high"* Hebrews 1:3.

Our cross – *"Whosoever will come after me, let him deny himself, and take up his cross, and follow me. For whosoever will save his life shall lose it; but whosoever shall lose his life for my sake and the gospel's, the same shall save it"* Mark 8:34-35.

The cure for man's sin-sick nature – *"I am come that they might have life, and that they might have it more abundantly"* John 10:10; *"In the world ye shall have tribulation: but be of good cheer; I have overcome the world"* John 16:33; *"But we all, with open face beholding as in a glass the glory of the Lord, are changed into the same image from glory to glory, even as by the Spirit of the Lord"* 2 Corinthians 3:18.

3. What must we do so that the will of God can be done in our lives? *(page 180)*

_____

II. That's My Dad! (Chapter 19)
    A. The legacy of a father is the ability he instills in his son and daughter. *(page 181)*   ___ True ___ False

        1. Check "True" or "False." Four responsibilities of society are: *(page 182)*
            a. To teach that traditional marriage is optional   ___ True ___ False
            b. To teach parents to love and care for their children   ___ True ___ False
            c. To strengthen families to strengthen the community   ___ True ___ False
            d. To teach children the importance of relationships   ___ True ___ False

        2. What is the leading indicator of the future of our nation? *(page 182)* _____
        Where should children receive their first instruction? _____

        3. Name three things a man's life is summed up in or founded upon. *(page 182)*

            _____

            _____

            _____

        4. Draw a line to the correct answer. *(pages 182-183)*
        Sons and daughters are   father a child.
        Fathers are   born.
        Any male can   made.
        Only a man can   conceive a child.

For Further Study:

Words of confession and contrition reveal an attitude of repentance and obedience – Psalm 51:3, 4; *"Create in me a new, clean heart, O God, filled with clean thoughts and right desires...make me willing to obey you"* Psalm 51:10, 12 TLB; *"He that covereth his sins shall not prosper: but whoso confesseth and forsaketh them shall have mercy"* Proverbs 28:13. Teach and train – Deuteronomy 6:5-9; 11:18-21 NIV; Colossians 3:16; 1 Thessalonians 4:1-8; 1 Timothy 3:4, 12 Who should teach – *"When I am old and greyheaded, O God, forsake me not; until I have shewed thy strength unto this generation, and thy power to every one that is to come"* Psalm 71:18; Proverbs 1:8, 9; 4:1; 6:20-24; 1 Timothy 1:18; 4:14. Examples to follow – Abraham: Genesis 18:19 NIV; Job: Job 29:11-25; Proverbs 20:11; 22:6, 15; 23:13; 31:10-31

5. Our responsibility is to raise trustworthy children who respect and admire _____.
    (circle one) (page 183)

    themselves   others   their father   a good-looking car

6. God's admonition to us is not to provoke our children to wrath but to *"bring them up in the nurture and admonition of the Lord."* Where is this Scripture found? _____

7. God gave the parents the responsibility to see that the children know the Lord. *(page 183)*
    ___ True ___ False

8. Name three things a father can teach his son. *(page 185)*

    _____

    _____

    _____

9. What is one of the most important things a father can teach his children? *(pages 186-187)*

    _____

    _____

    _____

10. What is the one gift that God gives a man and a woman that they can give one time to one person in one lifetime? *(page 187)* _____

For Further Study:

Trustworthy, obedient children – *"Set your hearts unto all the words which I testify among you this day, which ye shall command your children to observe to do, all the words of this law"* Deuteronomy 32:46; *"Children, obey your parents in the Lord: for this is right. Honour thy father and mother…That it may be well with thee, and thou mayest live long on the earth"* Ephesians 6:1; *"Children, obey your parents in all things: for this is wellpleasing unto the Lord"* Colossians 3:20; *"He must manage his own family well and see that his children obey him with proper respect"* 1 Timothy 3:4.

Ideal – *"Be their ideal; let them follow the way you teach and live; be a pattern for them in your love, your faith, and your clean thoughts"* 1 Timothy 4:12 TLB; *"Command and teach these things…Set an example…in speech, in life, in love, in faith and in purity…Devote yourself to the public reading of Scripture, to preaching and to teaching"* 1 Timothy 4:11-13 NIV; Titus 2:2-8.

11. What is the noblest calling on earth? *(page 187)* _____

12. The father in the home acts as _____ for the family. *(circle one) (page 188)*

    authoritarian   power   priest

13. No man has the right to talk to his children about God until he has talked to God about his children.
    (page 188) ___ True ___ False

III. Burn Out, Don't Fade Out (Chapter 20)
Match the following with the correct phrase: *(page 189)*

____ God loves you   a. from what you are.

____ He loves you too much to leave you   b. what you do.

____ People hear   c. the way you are.

____ People learn   d. what you say.

____ What you are is shown by   e. the way you are.

The difference between men who fail and those who succeed, more often than not, is their ability to handle _____. *(fill in the blank) (page 189)*

finances   pressure   promotion

For Further Study:

Important teaching assignment – *"I am praying that all is well with you and that your body is as healthy as I know your soul is…your life stays clean and true, and that you are living by the standards of the Gospel. I could have no greater joy than to hear such things about my children"* 3 John 1:2-4 TLB.

A test of manhood is handling pressure – *"You are a poor specimen if you can't stand the pressure of adversity"* Proverbs 24:10 TLB; *"If thou faint in the day of adversity, thy strength is small"* Proverbs 24:10; *"Blessed is the man who perseveres under trial, because when he has stood the test, he will receive the crown of life that God has promised to those who love him"* James 1:12 NIV.

God won't abandon you – *"For He [God] Himself has said, I will not in any way fail you nor give you up nor leave you without support. [I will] not…in any degree leave you helpless nor forsake nor let [you] down (relax My hold on you)! [Assuredly not!] So we take comfort and are encouraged and confidently and boldly say, The Lord is my Helper: I will not be seized with alarm [I will not fear or dread or be terrified]. What can man do to me?"* Hebrews 13:5, 6; Deuteronomy 31:6-8; Joshua 1:5, 6, 9; Psalms 27:1; 118:6.

Never quit – *"I press toward the mark for the prize of the high calling of God in Christ Jesus"* Philippians 3:13, 14.

Practical:

1. "What you believe about God shows what you believe about yourself." In prayer, ask God to show you what you need to change in how you see yourself and Him.

2. On the basis of what offering do we have God's mercy and grace to forgive us and reconcile us to Himself?

    _____

    Have you accepted that mercy and grace? If not, ask God to help you receive what He provided for you.

Repeat this prayer out loud:

Father, in the Name of Jesus, please help me to embrace all that You have provided for me through the Cross. Help me to see the magnitude of Your love for me and to understand how to "take everything to the Cross." Help me to show Your love to the children You have entrusted to my care and to take the responsibility for training them and bringing them up to know You. May Your love be reflected in me. Help me to be faithful to lift them up before You and then to lift You up before them. Thank You for Your mercy and grace. Amen.

For Further Study:

What you believe about God has the greatest potential for good or harm in your life – *"For I am not ashamed of the gospel of Christ: for it is the power of God unto salvation to every one that believeth"* Romans 1:16; *"Therefore if any man be in Christ, he is a new creature: old things are passed away; behold, all things are become new"* 2 Corinthians 5:17; *"Today if ye will hear his voice, Harden not your hearts"* Hebrews 3:7-8.

Always remember that God is for you, not against you – Psalm 56:9; *"For the Lord God is a sun and shield: the Lord will give grace and glory: no good thing will he withhold from them that walk uprightly"* Psalm 84:11; Romans 8:28, 38, 39.

God's Grace – *"In whom we have redemption through his blood, the forgiveness of sins, according to the riches of his grace"* Ephesians 1:7; *"For by grace are ye saved through faith; and that not of yourselves: it is the gift of God"* Ephesians 2:5-8; John 1:14-17; Acts 4:33; Titus 3:4-7.

God will help you – *"Know therefore that the Lord thy God, he is God, the faithful God, which keepeth covenant and mercy with them that love him and keep his commandments to a thousand generations"* Deuteronomy 7:9; *"So that we may boldly say, The Lord is my helper, and I will not fear what man shall do unto me"* Hebrews 13:6.

Self-Test *Lesson 12*

1. How did God display His love for the world? _____

2. What is the devil's lie? _____
   _____

3. Check "Yes" or "No" for the following statements about the Cross.

   ___ Yes ___ No   Jesus triumphed over principalities and powers.

   ___ Yes ___ No   Satan's power was increased.

   ___ Yes ___ No   We are crucified to the world.

   ___ Yes ___ No   The world is crucified to us.

4. What is the leading indicator of the future of our nation? _____

   Where should children receive their first instruction? _____

5. Name three things a man's life is summed up in or founded on.

   _____   _____   _____

6. Sons and daughters are _____.   Fathers are _____.

   Any male can _____.   Only a man can _____.

7. Name three things a father can teach his son.

   _____

   _____

   _____

8. What is the one gift that God gives a man and a woman that they can give one time to one person in one
   lifetime? _____

9. What is the noblest calling on earth? _____

10. No man has the right to talk to his children about God until he has talked to God about his children.

    ___ True ___ False

Keep this test for your own records.

Final Exam

1. What were the five sins that kept Israel out of Canaan?

   _____

   _____

   _____

   _____

   _____

2. What does Canaan Land represent for men today? _____
   _____

3. If a man cheats on his taxes and asks God to bless it, what sin is involved? *(circle one)*

   selfishness   tempting Christ   pride

4. Can a "maximized man" associate with people who murmur?   ___ Yes ___ No

5. In the process of psychologizing the Gospel, we eliminate the word _____.

6. Human sorrow for sin is based on being _____, while godly sorrow

   is based on _____.

7. Contrast human wisdom to godly wisdom. _____
   _____

8. Love centers in the: *(circle one)*

   will   heart   mind   emotions

9. What is the difference between an invitation and a command?

   _____

   _____

10. Unconfessed sin is unforgiven sin.   ___ True ___ False

11. Truth and reality are _____.

12. You'll never know the _____ of graduation until you've experienced the _____ of studying.

13. Unforgiveness _____ you to the sin of the one who has wronged you.

14. What commonly causes sins to pass from generation to generation? _____

15. Manhood and _____ are synonymous.

16. What God expects from men is _____.

17. Maturity doesn't come with _____ but with acceptance of _____.

18. No one can be responsible for success until he is willing to accept the responsibility for _____.

19. Prayer produces _____.

20. Every woman needs to know she is _____ to her man.

21. In relation to a wife, what does "appreciation" mean, and what does it produce?

    _____

    _____

22. You are _____ to what you confess.

23. If you do not treat your wife right, your _____ will not get ready answers.

24. One of the lowest levels of knowledge is: *(circle one)*

    assumption   kindergarten   street smarts

25. Self-justification makes you right in _____ eyes by placing _____ on someone else.

26. When something _____, it gains in value.

    When something _____, it loses in value.

27. When a woman is appreciated, she gains value in: *(circle as many as apply)*

    your eyes   her eyes   her children's eyes

DETACH HERE

28. If change doesn't come from the top, what will come from the bottom? _____

29. _____ is always the problem; _____ is always the solution.

30. Men often judge others by their _____ and themselves by their _____.

31. Some things in life are more important than _____.

32. The man is the _____ of the family.

33. Guilt leads to _____ which leads to _____.

34. There are times when silence is _____; other times it is just plain _____.

35. To reach your family, God looks to: *(circle one)*

    your wife   your church   you

36. The most powerful thing that can be done in life is to create an _____.

37. The degree of disappointment is found in the difference between the _____ and the _____.

38. Men's three-fold responsibility is to _____, _____ and _____.

39. Above all else, the greatest thing a father can do for his children is: *(circle one)*

    provide them gifts   love their mother   save for their future

40. Love is the desire to benefit _____ even at the expense of _____ because love desires to give.

41. What hour is one of the most important of a child's life? *(circle one)*

    dinner hour   study hour   video hour

42. One of the greatest thieves of family time is _____.

43. The _____ father is the curse of our day.

44. Listening is ministry.   ___ True ___ False

DETACH HERE

45. The fine print is part of _____. To minister to a woman, you must give her some

_____.

46. The sin of _____ is the basic sin of humanity.

47. The only reason you do _____ is because you don't do right.

48. Communication is the _____ of life.

49. When communication stops, _____ sets in.

50. The ultimate end of abnormality is _____.

51. It's harder to _____ than it is to _____.

52. One major reason for so much counseling today is because of: *(circle one)*

such a stressful society   so little prayer

so much divorce   the high cost of living

53. When the _____ wears off, you have nothing but _____ left.

54. The curse of our day is _____. Rather than being absent from the family, there is

an absence of _____ for the family.

55. Maturity doesn't come with age but begins with the acceptance of: *(circle one)*

leadership   a position   responsibility

56. Name a man's three options.

To be _____

To be _____

To be _____

57. Availability is not the greatest need in business or ministry, _____ is. *(circle one)*

education   teachability   a proven track record

58. The heart comes before the mind in telling us about our bodies and our lives. It is our heart more than our mind we should listen to. ___ True ___ False

59. What must you do to love God?

_____

60. Marriage is a _____, even as salvation is a _____ made with us through the shedding of Christ's blood on the Cross. A _____ is more than a contract. It's all a matter of the _____.

61. How did God display His love for the world? _____

62. What is the leading indicator of the future of our nation? _____
Where should children receive their first instruction? _____

63. Name three things a man's life is summed up in or founded on.

_____

_____

_____

64. Name three things a father can teach his son.

_____

_____

_____

65. What is the one gift that God gives a man and a woman that they can give one time to one person in one lifetime? _____

66. What is the noblest calling on earth? _____

67. No man has the right to talk to his children about God until he has talked to God about his children.
___ True ___ False

68. Short essay: The Bible says, *"Therefore to him that knoweth to do good and doeth it not, to him it is sin."* The sin of omission, not commission, creates the most problems for men. Explain how this can be, using personal illustrations and examples from the book.

_____

_____

_____

_____

_____

_____

_____

_____

_____

_____

Name _____

Address _____ City _____ State ____ Zip _____

Telephone a.m. _____ p.m. _____

Email Address _____

The Final Exam is required to be "commissioned."

For more information, contact
Christian Men's Network | P.O. Box 93478 | Southlake, TX 76092
www.cmnworld.com | cmnoffice@cmnworld.com

DETACH HERE

Basic Daily Bible Reading

Read Proverbs each morning for wisdom, Psalms each evening for courage. Make copies of this chart and keep it in your Bible to mark off as you read. If you are just starting the habit of Bible reading, be aware that longer translations or paraphrases (such as Amplified and Living) will take longer to read each day. As you start, it is okay to read only one of the chapters in Psalms each night, instead of the many listed. Mark your chart so you'll remember which ones you haven't read.
NOTE: The chronological chart following has the rest of the chapters of Psalms that are not listed here. By using both charts together, you will cover the entire book of Psalms.

Day of Month	Proverbs	Psalms	Day of Month	Proverbs	Psalms
1	1	1, 2, 4, 5, 6			
2	2	7, 8, 9	18	18	82, 83, 84, 85
3	3	10, 11, 12, 13, 14, 15	19	19	87, 88, 91, 92
4	4	16, 17, 19, 20	20	20	93, 94, 95, 97
5	5	21, 22, 23	21	21	98, 99, 100, 101, 103
6	6	24, 25, 26, 27	22	22	104, 108
7	7	28, 29, 31, 32	23	23	109, 110, 111
8	8	33, 35	24	24	112, 113, 114, 115, 117
9	9	36, 37	25	25	119:1-56
10	10	38, 39, 40	26	26	119:57-112
11	11	41, 42, 43, 45, 46	27	27	119:113-176
12	12	47, 48, 49, 50	28	28	120, 121, 122, 124, 130, 131, 133, 134
13	13	53, 55, 58, 61, 62			
14	14	64, 65, 66, 67	29	29	135, 136, 138
15	15	68, 69	30	30	139, 140, 141, 143
16	16	70, 71, 73	31	31	144, 145, 146, 148, 150
17	17	75, 76, 77, 81			

Chronological Annual Bible Reading

This schedule follows the events of the Bible chronologically and can be used with any translation or paraphrase of the Bible. Each day has an average of 77 verses of Scripture. If you follow this annually, along with your Daily Bible Reading, by your third year, you will recognize where you are and what is going to happen next. By your fifth year, you will understand the scriptural background and setting for any reference spoken of in a message or book. At that point, the Word will become more like "meat" to you and less like "milk." Once you understand the basic stories and what happens on the surface, God can reveal to you the layers of meaning beneath. So, make copies of this chart to keep in your Bible and mark off as you read. And start reading—it's the greatest adventure in life!

Some notes:
1. Some modern translations don't have verses numbered (such as The Message), so they cannot be used with this chart. Also, if you are just starting the Bible, be aware that longer translations or paraphrases (such as Amplified and Living) tend to take longer to read each day.
2. The Daily Bible Reading chart covers the Proverbs and the chapters of Psalms that are not listed here. By using both charts together, you will cover the entire books of Psalms and Proverbs along with the rest of the Bible.
3. The chronology of Scripture is obvious in some cases, educated guesswork in others. The placement of Job, for example, is purely conjecture since there is no consensus among Bible scholars as to its date or place. For the most part, however, chronological reading helps the reader, since it places stories that have duplicated information, or prophetic utterances elsewhere in Scripture, within the same reading sequence.

HOW TO READ SCRIPTURE NOTATIONS:
Book chapter: verse. (Mark 15:44 means the book of Mark, chapter 15, verse 44.)
Book chapter; chapter (Mark 15; 16; 17 means the book of Mark, chapters 15, 16, 17.)
Books continue the same until otherwise noted. (2 Kings 22; 23:1-28; Jeremiah 20 means the book of 2 Kings, chapter 22, the book of 2 Kings, chapter 23, verses 1-28; then the book of Jeremiah, chapter 20.)

1	Jan 1	Genesis 1; 2; 3
2	Jan 2	Genesis 4; 5; 6
3	Jan 3	Genesis 7; 8; 9
4	Jan 4	Genesis 10; 11; 12
5	Jan 5	Genesis 13; 14; 15; 16
6	Jan 6	Genesis 17; 18; 19:1-29
7	Jan 7	Genesis 19:30-38; 20; 21
8	Jan 8	Genesis 22; 23; 24:1-31
9	Jan 9	Genesis 24:32-67; 25
10	Jan 10	Genesis 26; 27
11	Jan 11	Genesis 28; 29; 30:1-24
12	Jan 12	Genesis 30:25-43; 31
13	Jan 13	Genesis 32; 33; 34
14	Jan 14	Genesis 35; 36
15	Jan 15	Genesis 37; 38; 39
16	Jan 16	Genesis 40; 41
17	Jan 17	Genesis 42; 43
18	Jan 18	Genesis 44; 45
19	Jan 19	Genesis 46; 47; 48
20	Jan 20	Genesis 49; 50; Exodus 1
21	Jan 21	Exodus 2; 3; 4
22	Jan 22	Exodus 5; 6; 7
23	Jan 23	Exodus 8; 9
24	Jan 24	Exodus 10; 11; 12
25	Jan 25	Exodus 13; 14; 15
26	Jan 26	Exodus 16; 17; 18
27	Jan 27	Exodus 19; 20; 21
28	Jan 28	Exodus 22; 23; 24
29	Jan 29	Exodus 25; 26
30	Jan 30	Exodus 27; 28; 29:1-28
31	Jan 31	Exodus 29:29-46; 30; 31
32	Feb 1	Exodus 32; 33; 34
33	Feb 2	Exodus 35; 36
34	Feb 3	Exodus 37; 38
35	Feb 4	Exodus 39; 40
36	Feb 5	Leviticus 1; 2; 3; 4
37	Feb 6	Leviticus 5; 6; 7
38	Feb 7	Leviticus 8; 9; 10
39	Feb 8	Leviticus 11; 12; 13:1-37
40	Feb 9	Leviticus 13:38-59; 14
41	Feb 10	Leviticus 15; 16
42	Feb 11	Leviticus 17; 18; 19
43	Feb 12	Leviticus 20; 21; 22:1-16
44	Feb 13	Leviticus 22:17-33; 23
45	Feb 14	Leviticus 24; 25
46	Feb 15	Leviticus 26; 27
47	Feb 16	Numbers 1; 2
48	Feb 17	Numbers 3; 4:1-20
49	Feb 18	Numbers 4:21-49; 5; 6
50	Feb 19	Numbers 7
51	Feb 20	Numbers 8; 9; 10
52	Feb 21	Numbers 11; 12; 13
53	Feb 22	Numbers 14; 15
54	Feb 23	Numbers 16; 17
55	Feb 24	Numbers 18; 19; 20
56	Feb 25	Numbers 21; 22
57	Feb 26	Numbers 23; 24; 25
58	Feb 27	Numbers 26; 27
59	Feb 28	Numbers 28; 29; 30
60	Mar 1	Numbers 31; 32:1-27
61	Mar 2	Numbers 32:28-42; 33
62	Mar 3	Numbers 34; 35; 36
63	Mar 4	Deuteronomy 1; 2
64	Mar 5	Deuteronomy 3; 4
65	Mar 6	Deuteronomy 5; 6; 7
66	Mar 7	Deuteronomy 8; 9; 10
67	Mar 8	Deuteronomy 11; 12; 13
68	Mar 9	Deuteronomy 14; 15; 16
69	Mar 10	Deuteronomy 17; 18; 19; 20
70	Mar 11	Deuteronomy 21; 22; 23
71	Mar 12	Deuteronomy 24; 25; 26; 27
72	Mar 13	Deuteronomy 28
73	Mar 14	Deuteronomy 29; 30; 31
74	Mar 15	Deuteronomy 32; 33
75	Mar 16	Deuteronomy 34; Psalm 90; Joshua 1; 2
76	Mar 17	Joshua 3; 4; 5; 6
77	Mar 18	Joshua 7; 8; 9
78	Mar 19	Joshua 10; 11
79	Mar 20	Joshua 12; 13; 14
80	Mar 21	Joshua 15; 16
81	Mar 22	Joshua 17; 18; 19:1-23
82	Mar 23	Joshua 19:24-51; 20; 21
83	Mar 24	Joshua 22; 23; 24
84	Mar 25	Judges 1; 2; 3:1-11
85	Mar 26	Judges 3:12-31; 4; 5
86	Mar 27	Judges 6; 7
87	Mar 28	Judges 8; 9
88	Mar 29	Judges 10; 11; 12
89	Mar 30	Judges 13; 14; 15
90	Mar 31	Judges 16; 17; 18
91	Apr 1	Judges 19; 20
		[You have completed 1/4 of the Bible!]
92	Apr 2	Judges 21; Job 1; 2; 3
93	Apr 3	Job 4; 5; 6
94	Apr 4	Job 7; 8; 9
95	Apr 5	Job 10; 11; 12
96	Apr 6	Job 13; 14; 15
97	Apr 7	Job 16; 17; 18; 19
98	Apr 8	Job 20; 21
99	Apr 9	Job 22; 23; 24
100	Apr 10	Job 25; 26; 27; 28
101	Apr 11	Job 29; 30; 31
102	Apr 12	Job 32; 33; 34
103	Apr 13	Job 35; 36; 37
104	Apr 14	Job 38; 39
105	Apr 15	Job 40; 41; 42
106	Apr 16	Ruth 1; 2; 3
107	Apr 17	Ruth 4; 1 Samuel 1; 2
108	Apr 18	1 Samuel 3; 4; 5; 6
109	Apr 19	1 Samuel 7; 8; 9
110	Apr 20	1 Samuel 10; 11; 12; 13
111	Apr 21	1 Samuel 14; 15
112	Apr 22	1 Samuel 16; 17
113	Apr 23	1 Samuel 18; 19; Psalm 59
114	Apr 24	1 Samuel 20; 21; Psalms 34; 56
115	Apr 25	1 Samuel 22; 23, Psalms 52; 142
116	Apr 26	1 Samuel 24; 25; 1 Chronicles 12:8-18; Psalm 57
117	Apr 27	1 Samuel 26; 27; 28; Psalms 54; 63
118	Apr 28	1 Samuel 29; 30; 31; 1 Chronicles 12:1-7; 12:19-22
119	Apr 29	1 Chronicles 10; 2 Samuel 1; 2
120	Apr 30	2 Samuel 3; 4; 1 Chronicles 11:1-9; 12:23-40
121	May 1	2 Samuel 5; 6; 1 Chronicles 13; 14
122	May 2	2 Samuel 22; 1 Chronicles 15
123	May 3	1 Chronicles 16; Psalm 18
124	May 4	2 Samuel 7; Psalms 96; 105
125	May 5	1 Chronicles 17; 2 Samuel 8; 9; 10
126	May 6	1 Chronicles 18; 19; Psalm 60; 2 Samuel 11
127	May 7	2 Samuel 12; 13; 1 Chronicles 20:1-3; Psalm 51
128	May 8	2 Samuel 14; 15
129	May 9	2 Samuel 16; 17; 18; Psalm 3
130	May 10	2 Samuel 19; 20; 21
131	May 11	2 Samuel 23:8-23
132	May 12	1 Chronicles 20:4-8; 11:10-25; 2 Samuel 23:24-39; 24
133	May 13	1 Chronicles 11:26-47; 21; 22
134	May 14	1 Chronicles 23; 24; Psalm 30
135	May 15	1 Chronicles 25; 26
136	May 16	1 Chronicles 27; 28; 29
137	May 17	1 Kings 1; 2:1-12; 2 Samuel 23:1-7
138	May 18	1 Kings 2:13-46; 3; 2 Chronicles 1:1-13
139	May 19	1 Kings 5; 6; 2 Chronicles 2
140	May 20	1 Kings 7; 2 Chronicles 3; 4
141	May 21	1 Kings 8; 2 Chronicles 5
142	May 22	1 Kings 9; 2 Chronicles 6; 7:1-10
143	May 23	1 Kings 10:1-13; 2 Chronicles 7:11-22; 8; 9:1-12; 1 Kings 4
144	May 24	1 Kings 10:14-29; 2 Chronicles 1:14-17; 9:13-28; Psalms 72; 127
145	May 25	Song of Solomon 1; 2; 3; 4; 5
146	May 26	Song of Solomon 6; 7; 8; 1 Kings 11:1-40
147	May 27	Ecclesiastes 1; 2; 3; 4
148	May 28	Ecclesiastes 5; 6; 7; 8
149	May 29	Ecclesiastes 9; 10; 11; 12; 1 Kings 11:41-43; 2 Chronicles 9:29-31
150	May 30	1 Kings 12; 2 Chronicles 10; 11
151	May 31	1 Kings 13; 14; 2 Chronicles 12
152	June 1	1 Kings 15: 2 Chronicles 13; 14; 15
153	June 2	1 Kings 16; 2 Chronicles 16; 17
154	June 3	1 Kings 17; 18; 19
155	June 4	1 Kings 20; 21
156	June 5	1 Kings 22; 2 Chronicles 18
157	June 6	2 Kings 1; 2; 2 Chronicles 19; 20; 21:1-3
158	June 7	2 Kings 3; 4
159	June 8	2 Kings 5; 6; 7
160	June 9	2 Kings 8; 9; 2 Chronicles 21:4-20
161	June 10	2 Chronicles 22; 23; 2 Kings 10; 11
162	June 11	Joel 1; 2; 3
163	June 12	2 Kings 12; 13; 2 Chronicles 24
164	June 13	2 Kings 14; 2 Chronicles 25; Jonah 1
165	June 14	Jonah 2; 3; 4; Hosea 1; 2; 3; 4
166	June 15	Hosea 5; 6; 7; 8; 9; 10
167	June 16	Hosea 11; 12; 13; 14

DETACH HERE

MAJORING IN MEN®

168	June 17	2 Kings 15:1-7; 2 Chronicles 26; Amos 1; 2; 3
169	June 18	Amos 4; 5; 6; 7
170	June 19	Amos 8; 9; 2 Kings 15:8-18; Isaiah 1
171	June 20	Isaiah 2; 3; 4; 2 Kings 15:19-38; 2 Chronicles 27
172	June 21	Isaiah 5; 6; Micah 1; 2; 3
173	June 22	Micah 4; 5; 6; 7; 2 Kings 16:1-18
174	June 23	2 Chronicles 28; Isaiah 7; 8
175	June 24	Isaiah 9; 10; 11; 12
176	June 25	Isaiah 13; 14; 15; 16
177	June 26	Isaiah 17; 18; 19; 20; 21
178	June 27	Isaiah 22; 23; 24; 25
179	June 28	Isaiah 26; 27; 28; 29
180	June 29	Isaiah 30; 31; 32; 33
181	June 30	Isaiah 34; 35; 2 Kings 18:1-8; 2 Chronicles 29
182	July 1	2 Chronicles 30; 31; 2 Kings 17; 2 Kings 16:19-20
		[You have completed 1/2 of the Bible!]
183	July 2	2 Kings 18:9-37; 2 Chronicles 32:1-19; Isaiah 36
184	July 3	2 Kings 19; 2 Chronicles 32:20-23; Isaiah 37
185	July 4	2 Kings 20; 21:1-18; 2 Chronicles 32:24-33; Isaiah 38; 39
186	July 5	2 Chronicles 33:1-20; Isaiah 40; 41
187	July 6	Isaiah 42; 43; 44
188	July 7	Isaiah 45; 46; 47; 48
189	July 8	Isaiah 49; 50; 51; 52
190	July 9	Isaiah 53; 54; 55; 56; 57
191	July 10	Isaiah 58; 59; 60; 61; 62
192	July 11	Isaiah 63; 64; 65; 66
193	July 12	2 Kings 21:19-26; 2 Chronicles 33:21-25; 34:1-7; Zephaniah 1; 2; 3
194	July 13	Jeremiah 1; 2; 3
195	July 14	Jeremiah 4; 5
196	July 15	Jeremiah 6; 7; 8
197	July 16	Jeremiah 9; 10; 11
198	July 17	Jeremiah 12; 13; 14; 15
199	July 18	Jeremiah 16; 17; 18; 19
200	July 19	Jeremiah 20; 2 Kings 22; 23:1-28
201	July 20	2 Chronicles 34:8-33; 35:1-19; Nahum 1; 2; 3
202	July 21	2 Kings 23:29-37; 2 Chronicles 35:20-27; 36:1-5; Jeremiah 22:10-17; 26; Habakkuk 1
203	July 22	Habakkuk 2; 3; Jeremiah 46; 47; 2 Kings 24:1-4; 2 Chronicles 36:6-7
204	July 23	Jeremiah 25; 35; 36; 45
205	July 24	Jeremiah 48; 49:1-33
206	July 25	Daniel 1; 2
207	July 26	Jeremiah 22:18-30; 2 Kings 24:5-20; 2 Chronicles 36:8-12; Jeremiah 37:1-2; 52:1-3; 24; 29
208	July 27	Jeremiah 27; 28; 23
209	July 28	Jeremiah 50; 51:1-19
210	July 29	Jeremiah 51:20-64; 49:34-39; 34
211	July 30	Ezekiel 1; 2; 3; 4
212	July 31	Ezekiel 5; 6; 7; 8

213	Aug 1	Ezekiel 9; 10; 11; 12
214	Aug 2	Ezekiel 13, 14, 15, 16:1-34
215	Aug 3	Ezekiel 16:35-63; 17; 18
216	Aug 4	Ezekiel 19; 20
217	Aug 5	Ezekiel 21; 22
218	Aug 6	Ezekiel 23; 2 Kings 25:1; 2 Chronicles 36:13-16; Jeremiah 39:1; 52:4; Ezekiel 24
219	Aug 7	Jeremiah 21; 22:1-9; 32; 30
220	Aug 8	Jeremiah 31; 33; Ezekiel 25
221	Aug 9	Ezekiel 29:1-16; 30; 31; 26
222	Aug 10	Ezekiel 27; 28; Jeremiah 37:3-21
223	Aug 11	Jeremiah 38; 39:2-10; 52:5-30
224	Aug 12	2 Kings 25:2-22; 2 Chronicles 36:17-21; Jeremiah 39:11-18; 40:1-6; Lamentations 1
225	Aug 13	Lamentations 2; 3
226	Aug 14	Lamentations 4; 5; Obadiah; Jeremiah 40:7-16
227	Aug 15	Jeremiah 41; 42; 43; 44; 2 Kings 25:23-26
228	Aug 16	Ezekiel 33:21-33; 34; 35; 36
229	Aug 17	Ezekiel 37; 38; 39
230	Aug 18	Ezekiel 32; 33:1-20; Daniel 3
231	Aug 19	Ezekiel 40; 41
232	Aug 20	Ezekiel 42; 43; 44
233	Aug 21	Ezekiel 45; 46; 47
234	Aug 22	Ezekiel 48; 29:17-21; Daniel 4
235	Aug 23	Jeremiah 52:31-34; 2 Kings 25:27-30; Psalms 44; 74; 79
236	Aug 24	Psalms 80; 86; 89
237	Aug 25	Psalms 102; 106
238	Aug 26	Psalms 123; 137; Daniel 7; 8
239	Aug 27	Daniel 5; 9; 6
240	Aug 28	2 Chronicles 36:22-23; Ezra 1; 2
241	Aug 29	Ezra 3; 4:1-5; Daniel 10; 11
242	Aug 30	Daniel 12; Ezra 4:6-24; 5; 6:1-13; Haggai 1
243	Aug 31	Haggai 2; Zechariah 1; 2; 3
244	Sept 1	Zechariah 4; 5; 6; 7; 8
245	Sept 2	Ezra 6:14-22; Psalm 78
246	Sept 3	Psalms 107; 116; 118
247	Sept 4	Psalms 125; 126; 128; 129; 132; 147
248	Sept 5	Psalm 149; Zechariah 9; 10; 11; 12; 13
249	Sept 6	Zechariah 14; Esther 1; 2; 3
250	Sept 7	Esther 4; 5; 6; 7; 8
251	Sept 8	Esther 9; 10; Ezra 7; 8
252	Sept 9	Ezra 9; 10; Nehemiah 1
253	Sept 10	Nehemiah 2; 3; 4; 5
254	Sept 11	Nehemiah 6; 7
255	Sept 12	Nehemiah 8; 9; 10
256	Sept 13	Nehemiah 11; 12
257	Sept 14	Nehemiah 13; Malachi 1; 2; 3; 4
258	Sept 15	1 Chronicles 1; 2:1-35
259	Sept 16	1 Chronicles 2:36-55; 3; 4
260	Sept 17	1 Chronicles 5; 6:1-41
261	Sept 18	1 Chronicles 6:42-81; 7
262	Sept 19	1 Chronicles 8; 9
263	Sept 20	Matthew 1; 2; 3; 4

264	Sept 21	Matthew 5; 6
265	Sept 22	Matthew 7; 8
266	Sept 23	Matthew 9; 10
267	Sept 24	Matthew 11; 12
268	Sept 25	Matthew 13; 14
269	Sept 26	Matthew 15; 16
270	Sept 27	Matthew 17; 18; 19
271	Sept 28	Matthew 20; 21
272	Sept 29	Matthew 22; 23
273	Sept 30	Matthew 24; 25
		[You have completed 3/4 of the Bible!]
274	Oct 1	Matthew 26; 27; 28
275	Oct 2	Mark 1; 2
276	Oct 3	Mark 3; 4
277	Oct 4	Mark 5; 6
278	Oct 5	Mark 7; 8:1-26
279	Oct 6	Mark 8:27-38; 9
280	Oct 7	Mark 10; 11
281	Oct 8	Mark 12; 13
282	Oct 9	Mark 14
283	Oct 10	Mark 15; 16
284	Oct 11	Luke 1
285	Oct 12	Luke 2; 3
286	Oct 13	Luke 4; 5
287	Oct 14	Luke 6; 7:1-23
288	Oct 15	Luke 7:24-50; 8
289	Oct 16	Luke 9
290	Oct 17	Luke 10; 11
291	Oct 18	Luke 12; 13
292	Oct 19	Luke 14; 15
293	Oct 20	Luke 16; 17
294	Oct 21	Luke 18; 19
295	Oct 22	Luke 20; 21
296	Oct 23	Luke 22
297	Oct 24	Luke 23; 24:1-28
298	Oct 25	Luke 24:29-53; John 1
299	Oct 26	John 2; 3; 4:1-23
300	Oct 27	John 4:24-54; 5; 6:1-7
301	Oct 28	John 6:8-71; 7:1-21
302	Oct 29	John 7:22-53; 8
303	Oct 30	John 9; 10
304	Oct 31	John 11; 12:1-28
305	Nov 1	John 12:29-50; 13; 14
306	Nov 2	John 15; 16; 17
307	Nov 3	John 18; 19:1-24
308	Nov 4	John 19:25-42; 20; 21
309	Nov 5	Acts 1; 2
310	Nov 6	Acts 3; 4
311	Nov 7	Acts 5; 6
312	Nov 8	Acts 7
313	Nov 9	Acts 8; 9
314	Nov 10	Acts 10
315	Nov 11	Acts 11
316	Nov 12	Acts 12; 13
317	Nov 13	Acts 14; 15; Galatians 1
318	Nov 14	Galatians 2; 3; 4
319	Nov 15	Galatians 5; 6; James 1
320	Nov 16	James 2; 3; 4; 5
321	Nov 17	Acts 16; 17
322	Nov 18	Acts 18:1-11; 1 Thessalonians 1; 2; 3; 4

DETACH HERE

323	Nov 19	1 Thessalonians 5;
		2 Thessalonians 1; 2; 3
324	Nov 20	Acts 18:12-28; 19:1-22;
		1 Corinthians 1
325	Nov 21	1 Corinthians 2; 3; 4; 5
326	Nov 22	1 Corinthians 6; 7; 8
327	Nov 23	1 Corinthians 9; 10; 11
328	Nov 24	1 Corinthians 12; 13; 14
329	Nov 25	1 Corinthians 15; 16
330	Nov 26	Acts 19:23-41; 20:1;
		2 Corinthians 1; 2
331	Nov 27	2 Corinthians 3; 4; 5
332	Nov 28	2 Corinthians 6; 7; 8; 9
333	Nov 29	2 Corinthians 10; 11; 12
334	Nov 30	2 Corinthians 13; Romans 1; 2
335	Dec 1	Romans 3; 4; 5
336	Dec 2	Romans 6; 7; 8
337	Dec 3	Romans 9; 10; 11

338	Dec 4	Romans 12; 13; 14
339	Dec 5	Romans 15; 16
340	Dec 6	Acts 20:2-38; 21
341	Dec 7	Acts 22; 23
342	Dec 8	Acts 24; 25; 26
343	Dec 9	Acts 27; 28
344	Dec 10	Ephesians 1; 2; 3
345	Dec 11	Ephesians 4; 5; 6
346	Dec 12	Colossians 1; 2; 3
347	Dec 13	Colossians 4; Philippians 1; 2
348	Dec 14	Philippians 3; 4; Philemon
349	Dec 15	1 Timothy 1; 2; 3; 4
350	Dec 16	1 Timothy 5; 6; Titus 1; 2
351	Dec 17	Titus 3; 2 Timothy 1; 2; 3
352	Dec 18	2 Timothy 4; 1 Peter 1; 2
353	Dec 19	1 Peter 3; 4; 5; Jude
354	Dec 20	2 Peter 1; 2; 3; Hebrews 1
355	Dec 21	Hebrews 2; 3; 4; 5

356	Dec 22	Hebrews 6; 7; 8; 9
357	Dec 23	Hebrews 10; 11
358	Dec 24	Hebrews 12; 13; 2 John; 3 John
359	Dec 25	1 John 1; 2; 3; 4
360	Dec 26	1 John 5; Revelation 1; 2
361	Dec 27	Revelation 3; 4; 5; 6
362	Dec 28	Revelation 7; 8; 9; 10; 11
363	Dec 29	Revelation 12; 13; 14; 15
364	Dec 30	Revelation 16; 17; 18; 19
365	Dec 31	Revelation 20; 21; 22

You have completed the entire Bible-Congratulations!

DETACH HERE

MAJORING IN MEN® CURRICULUM

MANHOOD GROWTH PLAN

*Order the corresponding workbook for each book, and study the first four Majoring In Men®
Curriculum books in this order:*

MAXIMIZED MANHOOD: Realize your need for God in every area of your life and start
mending relationships with Christ and your family.

COURAGE: Make peace with your past, learn the power of forgiveness and the value of character.
Let yourself be challenged to speak up for Christ to other men.

COMMUNICATION, SEX AND MONEY: Increase your ability to communicate, place the
right values on sex and money in relationships, and greatly improve relationships, whether
married or single.

STRONG MEN IN TOUGH TIMES: Reframe trials, battles and discouragement in light of
Scripture and gain solid footing for business, career, and relational choices in the future.

*Choose five of the following books to study next. When you have completed nine books, if you are
not in men's group, you can find a Majoring In Men® group near you and become "commissioned"
to minister to other men.*

DARING: Overcome fear to live a life of daring ambition for Godly pursuits.

SEXUAL INTEGRITY: Recognize the sacredness of the sexual union, overcome mistakes and
blunders and commit to righteousness in your sexuality.

THE UNIQUE WOMAN: Discover what makes a woman tick, from adolescence through
maturity, to be able to minister to a spouse's uniqueness at any age.

NEVER QUIT: Take the ten steps for entering or leaving any situation, job, relationship or crisis
in life.

REAL MAN: Discover the deepest meaning of Christlikeness and learn to exercise good character in times of stress, success or failure.

POWER OF POTENTIAL: Start making solid business and career choices based on Biblical principles while building core character that affects your entire life.

ABSOLUTE ANSWERS: Adopt practical habits and pursue Biblical solutions to overcome "prodigal problems" and secret sins that hinder both success and satisfaction with life.

TREASURE: Practice Biblical solutions and principles on the job to find treasures such as the satisfaction of exercising integrity and a job well done.

IRRESISTIBLE HUSBAND: Avoid common mistakes that sabotage a relationship and learn simple solutions and good habits to build a marriage that will consistently increase in intensity for decades.

MAJORING IN MEN® CURRICULUM

CHURCH GROWTH PLAN
STRONG - SUSTAINABLE - SYNERGISTIC
THREE PRACTICAL PHASES TO A POWERFUL MEN'S MOVEMENT IN YOUR CHURCH

Phase One:

- Pastor disciples key men/men's director using Maximized Manhood system.

- Launch creates momentum among men

- Church becomes more attractive to hold men who visit

- Families grow stronger

- Men increase bond to pastor

Phase Two:

- Men/men's director teach other men within the church

- Increased tithing and giving by men

- Decreased number of families in crisis

- Increased mentoring of teens and children

- Increase of male volunteers

- Faster assimilation for men visitors - clear path for pastor to connect with new men

- Men pray regularly for pastor

Phase Three:

- Men teach other men outside the church and bring them to Christ

- Increased male population and attraction to a visiting man, seeing a place he belongs

- Stronger, better-attended community outreaches

- Men are loyal to and support pastor

This system enables the pastor to successfully train key leaders,

create momentum, build a church that attracts and holds men

who visit, and disciple strong men.

Churches may conduct men's ministry entirely free of charge!

Learn how by calling 817-437-4888.

CONTACT
MAJORING IN MEN® CURRICULUM
817-437-4888
office@ChristianMensNetwork.com

Christian Men's Network
P.O. Box 3
Grapevine, TX 76099

Great discounts available!

Start your discipleship TODAY!
Receive 20% off your first order at CMN.men
by calling 817-437-4888.

ABOUT THE AUTHOR

Edwin Louis Cole mentored hundreds of thousands of people through challenging events and powerful books that have become the most widely-used Christian men's resources in the world. He is known for pithy statements and a confrontational style that demanded social responsibility and family leadership.

After serving as a pastor, evangelist, and Christian television pioneer, and at an age when most men were retiring, he followed his greatest passion—to lead men into Christlikeness, which he called "real manhood."

Ed Cole was a real man through and through. A loving son to earthly parents and the heavenly Father. Devoted husband to the "loveliest lady in the land," Nancy Corbett Cole. Dedicated father to three and, over the years, accepting the role of "father" to thousands. A reader, a thinker, a visionary. A man who made mistakes, learned lessons, then shared the wealth of his wisdom with men around the world. The Christian Men's Network he founded in 1977 is still a vibrant, global ministry. Unquestionably, he was the greatest men's minister of his generation.

CMN.men
@ChristianMensNetwork
@EdwinLouisCole